WHEN DAVE WENT UP

Gary Jordan

WHEN DAVE WENT UP

The Inside Story of Wimbledon's 1988 FA Cup Win

First published by Pitch Publishing, 2023

Pitch Publishing
9 Donnington Park,
85 Birdham Road,
Chichester,
West Sussex,
PO20 7AJ
www.pitchpublishing.co.uk
info@pitchpublishing.co.uk

A CIP catalogue record is available for this book
from the British Library.

ISBN 978 1 80150 443 0

Typesetting and origination by Pitch Publishing

Printed and bound in Great Britain by TJ Books, Padstow

Contents

This book is dedicated to all those who chose to believe, and even those who didn't.

Dream big, and great things happen.

Introduction

WHEN I first started going to games in 1986, I was fortunate to be joining at just the right time of supporting the Dons. Of course, any time is a good time, but at this moment it was a peak time. Sure, we'd had our big days as a non-league team, some of which are documented in this book. Wimbledon had just reached the very top though, quite literally, and so I felt honoured to have First Division football on my doorstep, and then a trip to Wembley just a few months later – it doesn't get much better than that.

This book will take you on a trip back to 1988, and even further, because I feel our history is rich with moments that some will perhaps recall even more vividly than the FA Cup win. So this is as much for them, and their heroes, as it is for the ones I grew up with. Also, there are those who have witnessed finals in the modern era, who will have had stories told to them, by family and friends of how they were there. An omission in editing was the fact that Lawrie Sanchez said he must have met 80,000 Wimbledon fans who were there that day. We all have a story to tell, but this is the players' story, and those who helped them become the club legends that they are.

You will notice that during certain parts of the book there will be discrepancies regarding some events. Over 30 years have passed since winning the FA Cup so clearly some elements will have differing versions of what actually happened, or opinions. I have done my best to piece this together to make it the best version of the team, season, cup run, and everything in between. It is a big puzzle that may have edges that have become a bit rough and will not fit the picture that you remember.

The players who have contributed to the book, as well as journalists, and even a referee, have given up their time to help recreate the story as best they can, for you, the fan, to enjoy.

One

1975

THE WORLD of non-league football is vast. Some team names are instantly recognisable and others will have fleeting glimpses of moments as national headlines, caused of course by the glamour of the FA Cup. As each round is successfully navigated, a new challenge is drawn up.

The velvet bag, with the Football Association logo embroidered carefully on to its side, would entice many exciting moments as the now long-gone tradition of tuning in to a radio soon after the previous round's games had been played out, all on a Saturday as well, to hear the balls clacking around as they are taken out one-by-one, in the hope that your team would get a favourable draw, or that dream tie against a top-division side. The draws for the early rounds were not broadcast live, and you would have to wait for word of mouth to know who you would face next, such was the non-existence of mobile phones, the internet, or the whirlpool of social media.

Wimbledon were just like any other team in the mid-1970s, in that they would ply their trade in their regional divisions, gaining promotion, avoiding relegation, and keeping the books ticking over. A bonus would be a cup run, either at amateur level, or if a team was lucky enough getting past the qualifying rounds of the FA Cup to have that moment in the sun – although as the early rounds were played through the winter months, it would be the biting wind and heavy mud-covered pitches, rather than warm sunshine.

Allen Batsford took charge of the Dons in the summer of 1974, coming from another amateur club, the smaller but well-known Walton & Hersham. Two seasons before his arrival at Plough Lane he had successfully taken them to FA Amateur Cup glory at Wembley, the Swans beating Slough Town 1-0. During that same season he took Walton to the second round of the FA Cup, having beaten Bristol City of the Fourth Division in the first round proper, and they also finished as runners-up in the Isthmian League. Then, the following season they took Brighton & Hove Albion to a replay in the second round, where they then dispatched the professional outfit 4-0. Making this even more special was the fact that Brian Clough managed the Seagulls.

Batsford was a student of the game and was always looking at ways to bring new tactics into his way of playing. Allied with a thorough discipline regime, his teams were always tough to beat first, and then could play the game as he wanted. His approach to his players was of loyalty and respect, knowing that if he treated them as equals, they would perform for him on matchdays. To say Batsford's stock was high is an understatement, and so the Dons swooped and got their man to help kick-start a new era for the club. After nine years with the Swans, it was time for Batsford to dip his toes into a new pond and after two interviews he was offered the job.

That was the easy part; assembling a team on a shoestring budget was the real challenge, as he admitted, 'There were just six players at the time, so I had to bring in people I knew. I brought in five from Walton & Hersham and I was fortunate the two sets of players gelled.' The roll of the dice worked and even though Batsford was not fully aware of their playing ability he was positive that with hard work the new squad could achieve remarkable things. He was particularly impressed by schoolteacher Mick Mahon, and thought he was of league standard. Also, Ian Cooke was singled out for praise early on.

It was an instant transformation and the five Walton players who arrived with the new boss went straight into the opening-day fixture, a 2-0 loss at Nuneaton Borough. 'We gave away a couple of silly goals,' said one of the new recruits, Dave Donaldson. 'I wasn't sure that I'd made the right move. Selwyn Rice was sent off and the team was totally disjointed. Looking at the game you would never have predicted what was to follow.' Instead of feeling sorry for themselves the Dons went on a run of 11 consecutive league wins, and mixed into that was the start of the FA Cup run that is still talked about now as one of the greatest by any non-league team ever.

Saturday, 14 September 1974 is not a date that football historians will know well. In fact it is a nondescript date in football. This, though, was the day that *the run* started, and against that famous name of Bracknell Town. Yes, this is where history would start. Spartan League Bracknell had started the season brightly and were unbeaten, compared to the Dons' one defeat. The first qualifying round and the visit of Wimbledon saw a crowd just short of 1,000 witnessing a tie that got off to a fast start. Keiron Somers let fly a blockbuster of a shot after decent work by Mick Mahon on the left. Somers would have thought his effort was in, but Steve McLurg managed to get his head to the ball, which in turn deflected the goalbound effort on to the bar. This was just the opening minute and shortly after that the Dons were behind. The rural setting of Larges Lane was cheering loud when John Adams connected with a long Alan Jeffries free kick, the striker getting to the ball marginally ahead of Dickie Guy.

Bracknell had their tails up and soon after could have doubled their lead. Adams linked up with his strike partner Norman Budd, and after a swift exchange of passes Budd was clean through only to blaze his shot over the bar. A let-off, and further warning that the FA Cup for this season could be over before it even truly began. The Dons started to up their game. Somers and Roger Connell started to cause problems for the Bracknell defence, but it was Ian Cooke who had the first real chance to level the scores, with a fine run and shot that saw Ron Gurney in the home goal save at full length. The equaliser did come and on the 20-minute mark it was Cooke who got the goal. Mahon swung over a deep corner, Somers nodded back across the goal and Cooke was ready to put his header into the net.

Now in the ascendency, it did not take long for Wimbledon to go ahead for the first time in the game. This was all about the power and agility of Connell, with the help of a full-back. Bob Stockley was getting some freedom and making overlapping runs with regularity, then on half an hour he chipped a cross over for Connell who headed goalward only to see the ball come back off the post, and despite being on the floor he recovered his feet enough to stab the rebound home.

The game was all but up by half-time with a third Dons goal, and Connell's second, making the most of an injury to the Bracknell captain who was receiving treatment for a shoulder injury. The bearded sharp-shooter was starting to take control of the game and despite being off target shortly after putting the Dons ahead he was ready when Stockley and Cooke combined again to set him up. Cooke chased what looked a lost cause, with Stockley's ball going to the corner flag. He somehow worked his way around his defender to place a perfect cross over for an easy header which Connell duly despatched.

Bracknell now had nothing to lose and did all they could to cut the deficit. Wimbledon were making life difficult for themselves and Dave Donaldson dithered on the ball, almost allowing Rudd a chance. Worse was to come with 15 minutes left when Guy and Billy Edwards got in a mess with Rudd in on goal again. This brought some remonstrations from Batsford on the sideline and the sharp words seemed to steady the boat a little. Guy was called upon again a couple more times, but the final whistle came with some relief. This had been a test and proved that as keen as the Dons were, they had to be at their best if they were to have the continued dream of a big name coming out with them in the draw.

For the next round on 5 October, Maidenhead United were the visitors – not necessarily a big name but at least there was no travelling this time as the tie would be played at Plough Lane. The run-up to the game was not exactly smooth. Dave Lucas was sidelined with a muscle injury, Mick Mahon was out with fibrositis, and in a weird late twist new signing Glen Aitken was also forced out but for quite different reasons. Aitken had recently been acquired from Gillingham and was named in the side to play the Isthmian League Second Division outfit, when just five minutes before kick-off the club learned that the registration of the signing had not been cleared. With a mild panic setting in it was known that Malcolm Swain, who had just completed a month's trial loan from Reading, was in the ground; more precisely in the bar! After a sprint to his car to grab his boots and get his kit on, the game could start. Again, the front pair of Connell and Somers would be too much for the opposition, and despite holding on for the first half an hour the Maidenhead goal was finally breached. Eddie Junger was keeping his side in the game early on with fine saves, most notably from Connell as the striker turned deftly and cracked a vicious shot which was kept out by the full-stretch Maidenhead stopper. It was Connell's strength that proved decisive for the opener, as he rode a hefty challenge to stay upright and unleash a powerful shot that went in at the near post.

At just 1-0 up by half-time the Dons had to be on their toes as Maidenhead started the second period brightly, but nerves were calmed when Edwards, who had earlier almost created a goal for Cooke, combined with Cooke again to provide an opening for Somers who neatly scored with his left foot. The third goal had some flair to treat the crowd of over 1,300. A free kick on the edge of the penalty area saw Dave Bassett knock the ball through Swain's legs and Connell rifled home his shot. The fourth was from an error in Maidenhead's defence as Stockley's low cross somehow evaded everyone and Connell was on hand to complete his hat-trick. There was almost a fifth, but Bassett saw his header thump off the bar.

Two weeks later the Dons had another home draw, this time against Wokingham Town, another Isthmian Second Division team. To their credit Wokingham stuck to their task and held the Dons to half chances, despite the home team's dominance. Another healthy crowd of just over 1,500 then witnessed the tie turn in confusing and controversial circumstances just before the interval. Stockley was again marauding down the line and his cross went over the target of Somers, and Dixon in the goal caught the ball as Cooke came in to challenge. Play was to continue, but the referee noticed his linesman waving his flag on the sideline. 'I wasn't in a position to see it myself, but my linesman was in a perfect place,' said Mr M.G. Richardson. 'The keeper took the ball over the line as he went to throw it out.' This was the official's explanation after the game, and Stockley, who had crossed the ball, was given credit for the goal. There have been more bizarre goals but this one broke the resolve of the visitors at a crucial point in the game.

Wimbledon then put the tie to bed early in the second half. Mahon had already threatened to double their lead when he struck the underside of the bar after great link-up play by Connell and Somers. Then just a couple of minutes later Cooke did get the second as he was on hand to convert a loose ball after Somers' header at goal. The only blot on this game's copybook came halfway through the second half when a penalty was awarded to the Dons after a handball. Mahon took it but his shot was too weak, and Dixon was able to save easily. Despite the Dons hitting the bar twice within a minute with around ten to play, the match was already won and now Wimbledon had one more hurdle to jump before that dream tie.

Again, it was a fortnight between games, and into early November for the fourth qualifying round. The Dons, who were rolling in the league, carried the form into their cup games. The final qualifying round sent the Dons away to Guildford & Dorking United, who were struggling in the same Southern League that Batsford's side were flying in. In fact, they had met just a few weeks before at the same venue, and a Cooke hat-trick and Mahon brace saw the Dons run out comfortable winners, but it had taken four goals in the last 15 minutes to see the game off. And this was remarkably similar. Just over 1,200 were on hand to witness what was mostly a run-of-the-mill match. It was reported that the atmosphere was severely lacking that of a game which had such a potential big prize at the end of it, although this did not bother the Dons as they opened the scoring in the first ten minutes. Connell, who else in this run so far, netted with a header from a cross by Mahon, who else again, which flew past Alan Spratley in the Guildford goal. This allowed Wimbledon to ease off a bit but remain alert and wary to any danger. The home side did grow into the game but lacked any clinical thrust, and Guy only had routine saves to make, especially as the ground was slick after some rain before and during the early part of the game. Guy did have a moment when he let a shot slip away from him only to thankfully see it rebound back off a post. Connell was a constant threat, and if Guildford had a striker with even half of his ability the tie could have been different. As it was, Connell was toying with the hosts' defence as he plundered a shot at Spratley who could not hold on but had the rebound put out for a corner.

Wimbledon, with one foot in the first round, were taking their time putting their opponents out of their misery but were showing a bit more bite in the second half. Guildford, despite being just a goal down, were showing no real effort to get back into the tie, and therefore it was inevitable that Wimbledon would make their dominance count. With Somers and Connell a constant threat, and uncharacteristically missing chances, it was some pressure by Connell that led to a mistake by Alan Wright in defence. The striker headed the ball beyond him and Donaldson, who was keeping up with play, applied the finishing touch. That was with five minutes to go, and in the last minute of the contest it was Ian Cooke who got his reward for another outstanding performance. Latching on to a Somers header, he drilled a shot across the goal into the far corner. The scoreline flattered a little as the Dons were not at their best but they had done enough to score three times and put themselves in the draw, with the chance to put their fine run of form, currently 16 unbeaten at this stage, up against a Football League side.

The first round proper did not offer the 'glamour' everyone at the club had wished for. Instead they were handed a tricky home match against Bath City. Also in the Southern League, Bath had started the season well, but Wimbledon were on a huge 20-game winning streak. The Dons were simply beating everyone they came up against, in all competitions. A huge crowd at Plough Lane, helped with some games being called off locally, was close to 5,500. Wimbledon were now starting to make people sit up and take notice, as scoring goals and winning games attracts crowds; add the bonus of FA Cup action and why would you not want to see what was happening? Allen Batsford was assembling a team ready to make Wimbledon famous for something other than the tennis championships up the road each summer.

Bath had set their stall out early and their manager, Bert Head, had organised his team well. The defence had been tasked with keeping the free-scoring Connell quiet and playing counter-attacking football. Wimbledon stuck to their guns and even though the pitch was heavy they were always looking for that killer pass to break the Bath resistance. Selwyn Rice was conducting the team in midfield like it was his own personal orchestra. Moving the ball around, with fierce tackling and endless running, he really was the key instrument as well as conductor. There were early chances, and Cooke should have done better when played in on goal by Somers, but he miskicked his effort. Bath looked dangerous on the counter, boasting ex-Arsenal winger Alan Skirton in their ranks, and Bryant had to be alert to clear a cross for a corner. His game was cut short by injury though and this meant one less threat to worry over. Bath were forced to change their tactics and they reverted to a more defensive shape.

This invited Wimbledon on more and on the hour they nearly got the opening goal. Cooke did well to create space for himself but his shot fizzed past the post. Soon after that Bassett's shot was smartly saved. Then it was Guy's time to save as he kept out a great Tinson header. With the game entering the final ten minutes it seemed as if the Bath plan would work, and a replay would be played in the west country, but there was late drama as an indirect free kick was awarded to the Dons after Connell was obstructed. His touch from the set play to Mahon, however, was deflected harmlessly back in to play. Then with the clock reaching 90 minutes the fairy-tale cup tie finish for any schoolboy happened.

No one could quite believe what they witnessed and to this day it is a shot that lives in folklore for those who were there to see it. Mahon did not hesitate when a loose ball came his way at least 35 yards out. Often these distances get exaggerated over time, like the stuff of legend, but this was so far out, further than you would think possible. Tired legs did not come into it as Mahon hit the ball with such pace and power, and it went as true as an arrow into the Bath goal. It remains one of the single best moments of a

Wimbledon match – just ask anyone who was there. It put the Dons into the second round.

Kettering Town were the next FA Cup visitors to Plough Lane, and having beaten Swansea City 3-1 in the previous round their confidence was high. The form they carried over from the Southern League was also good so this was the toughest test yet on their run. Almost 6,000 fans came through the turnstiles just 11 days before Christmas, the biggest crowd for 11 seasons. The Dons' unbeaten run now stood at 24 and both teams fancied their chances of progression, which would mean a place in the third round for the first time for Wimbledon. As other teams had done before them, Kettering set up defensively with the hope of snatching a goal on the break. This only allowed Wimbledon the space needed to apply endless pressure on their goal.

Eventually, after a fast start, the first goal of the game came. Cooke, who had been a huge influence in the campaign so far, later said of his header after 13 minutes, 'It's always nice to see them go in like that, especially when it's something we have rehearsed in training.' Captain Cooke was full of praise for his team, 'I think we played quite well and deserved our 2-0 lead at half-time.'

The second came on 37 minutes when Mahon, who had provided the cross for his skipper to open the scoring, converted a penalty won by the persistent play of Connell. The Kettering goalkeeper Gordon Livsey tripped up the attacker after he let the ball run loose after a back-pass and Mahon put away the spot kick with ease. The game did not pass off without incident as Stockley was booked for a two-fingered gesture towards the away fans who had been giving him some stick. This was after he won the free kick that led to the opening goal. It was a shame that Kettering had shown up to play so defensively; in fact it was very naive given the amount of goals Wimbledon were capable of scoring. It was just a matter of time before they did so again. Once they had the lead the game was over as a contest.

History was made and Batsford had more than delivered already in his brief time at the club. 'At no time did I think we were going to lose. They [Kettering] didn't put us under anywhere near the same sort of pressure that Bath did in the last round,' the manager said. At this point though no one really cared as the draw for the next round was imminent, and surely this time Wimbledon would get their reward for such an impressive assault in the competition.

First Division Burnley, at Turf Moor. At last! The big time really had come calling. Granted, it was not the biggest fish in the pond, but they had decent players in their side, such as Brian Flynn, Ray Hankin, Paul Fletcher and Leighton James. This was just the tie that all Dons players, and fans, had hoped for. It was a chance to highlight their talent and togetherness.

For Allen Batsford this was a chance to pit his tactical nous against a team from the top table of English football.

Knowing how the opposition set up and played was key to Batsford's approach. He and coach Brian Hall set their own plans out during a training session just hours before the game. Fresh in the minds of the players, they created a blueprint which the team turned into a masterpiece of planning. Wins like this do not just happen – this was a team that was eighth in the First Division and complacency played a part in their thinking. Nevertheless, with the way Wimbledon played the game they deserved the win. One goal was enough to decide the tie, and once again it was Mahon who provided the magic. 'I thought Roger Connell was going to get in the way, but luckily he didn't, and I just hit it with my left foot,' he said. The ball went through a crowd of players in the box and ended up safely in the goal.

Mahon added, 'I wasn't even sure it went it. I never saw it hit the net!' Skipper Ian Cooke was amazed that the top-flight club's staff did not make any changes during the game as they were being beaten to everything aerially, 'Burnley should have spotted that their forwards were not winning the ball in the air. They really underestimated us.' Dickie Guy had to be on his toes a few times, but nowhere near as much as he would have anticipated before the game. It was his opposite number who was being tested more frequently and although the England under-23 stopper Alan Stevenson was equal to most things that came his way he could only parry Cooke's effort in the 49th minute into the path of Mahon. It was the first time since Darlington in the 1920s that a non-league team had beaten a First Division side. Burnley defender Peter Noble was clearly dejected but also praised his amateur counterparts, 'I know what it must feel like for Wimbledon but let's face it, we want shooting.'

Batsford had done his homework and identified that Welsh international Leighton James would be Burnley's main threat, so he doubled up on him with Stockley and Bassett. The final whistle was greeted with whooping and hollering. Perhaps this was the first twinkling of a Crazy Gang, and as the pre-purchased champagne started to flow – was that confidence or simply good preparation? – the manager told reporters, 'Absolutely marvellous. But we should never really have put a First Division side out of the cup.'

With the game won all ears turned to the radio and the draw for the next round. Surely any draw now could not top this one, and if it did would Wimbledon be able to repeat their dramatics? Of the Dons' next opponents, Batsford then said, 'Couldn't be better. Last year I thought they were the finest team in the land. But now we feel we can go there and do well.' Who was he referring to? Leeds. Leeds United.

Having beaten the top Lancashire side, the Dons would now travel to Yorkshire, to Elland Road and a team packed full of international footballers. 'Leeds are such a worldly team. But we shall be going there to make it as difficult as possible for them, and we shall probably ask advice from a First Division club again,' said Ian Cooke, who was sure that Leeds would be more aware of the south Londoners after this huge upset, 'I don't think Leeds will underestimate us as much as Burnley did.' And this was ratified by their manager Jimmy Armfield: 'We must treat them [Wimbledon] as professionals and not get complacent and underestimate the opposition. It will be important to be in the right frame of mind.'

And so came 25 January and the journey to Elland Road and infamy. In front of over 46,000 fans – including 2,000 hardy Dons followers – the largest crowd of the fourth round, another footballing miracle occurred. This time Wimbledon did not win the match but they did win the hearts and minds of the nation with a backs-to-the-wall performance that repelled everything the mighty Leeds could throw at them. Goalkeeper Dickie Guy was in outstanding form and even had the audacity to save a penalty with less than ten minutes left in the contest. It was one of those days that come around once in a generation. If Batsford thought that Wimbledon should never have defeated First Division Burnley, then he sure knew how to play down the odds of his team.

'I don't usually save many penalties,' Guy said in the aftermath of what he had achieved with his team-mates. 'I made up my mind a week ago that if Peter Lorimer took a penalty I'll go to my right. Most of the blasters who have taken them against me put it that side.' Lorimer was exactly that, a blaster of the ball, whether it be from the spot or open play. This time, although struck well, it was not the Scot's best penalty. 'It's worth missing all the others to have stopped this one,' Guy grinned. 'Perhaps I was saving up for it.' With time remaining in the game Guy was still busy and could not bask in his glory moment. Leeds, fuelled by the miss, or rather save, piled forward but Guy would not let anything past him. This was a team that had only conceded one goal so far in the entire run, in the fourth minute all the way back in their first tie at Bracknell. That seemed a long time ago now as Guy flew across his line and denied Eddie Gray, Johnny Giles and Gordon McQueen with some point-blank saves. 'I don't remember much about the final whistle. I just got to the dressing room and anyone who was anyone was there. I was dragged out to face the media. I had to have a swig of brandy to calm myself down!' recalled Guy. He was later to be interviewed by the BBC and then after staying over in Leeds for the night, he travelled back to London with his wife in an ITV car, as he was booked in to be part of *The Big Match*, hosted by Brian Moore. 'It was the highlight of my career,' Guy said.

As much as this game will be known for Guy's heroics, it could also have been a day for Keiron Somers as he turned down the opportunity of a square pass to play in Cooke or Connell. Instead, he attempted to take on one too many men and his chance went begging. The closest the Dons came to a goal was when Billy Edwards' well-struck shot hit the post. All the Wimbledon players on this day were heroes and it's wrong to single too many out, but there was some outstanding work in defence by Selwyn Rice until he had to leave the game early in the second half, to be replaced by Glen Aitken. Rice said, 'I just had a shot. [Billy] Bremner left his tackle a bit late when he got me. It was the first kick he'd had until then! When I got to the other end of the field there was blood all over the place.' After receiving several painkilling injections, the gash would require three stitches.

Batsford kept his cool over the penalty decision – it was an obvious foul by Bassett on Eddie Gray – but after the game had some harsh words about the horror tackle, 'Bremner went over the ball. What amazed me is that the ref saw it, told Bremner off but didn't give a free kick. It makes a nonsense of things.' Leeds were very ponderous in their approach play, and even though they respected the Dons they never really enjoyed any sustained pressure until the panic of not getting their desired result started to set in. 'We gave the ball away too much in midfield,' Armfield rued afterwards. There were harsh words said in the home team dressing room after the game, but already more plans were being made for the replay after this fascinating cup tie ended goalless. And to think that Wimbledon did this without the services of the talismanic Micky Mahon, who missed out due to being stricken with flu.

The defending First Division champions had another chance to 'ease through' to the next round, such were the words of former boss Don Revie, and Brian Clough, who had of course been beaten by a Batsford team before. This, though, was a different chapter, in an altogether different story. The replay was originally planned for Plough Lane but was moved to Crystal Palace's Selhurst Park ground, such was the demand for tickets, a decision that was not taken easily. When tickets initially went on sale they soon sold out and fears of touts and forgeries meant the safest option was to relocate the tie to the neighbours' larger ground, coupled with a very waterlogged pitch which led to it being delayed for a few days.

An even bigger crowd was in attendance to see a goalless first half which kept the impossible a reality, although it was almost a dream start as inside the first minute Somers had an effort cleared off the line by Terry Yorath, and then Rice forced David Harvey into a super save. Still inside the first five minutes, Connell let the occasion get to him after he dispossessed Yorath inside the area only to fire his shot well wide of the goal. With the early flurry of chances gone it was Leeds who started to come into the game and push the Dons back on to their heels, but the stubborn defence did not yield. That was until the 50th minute when Bassett, who had given away the penalty in the first game, was not so lucky this time as a wild Johnny Giles shot deflected wickedly off the defender and gave Guy no chance of stopping the ball going in. 'It wasn't the hardest of shots. I was in line with it and all I heard was

Dickie Guy shouting "Keeper!" So, I turned sideways to move out the way,' Bassett recalled. 'But I just couldn't get my left knee out of the way in time and the ball hit it and went in the other corner.'

It would have been forgiven if Wimbledon had folded at this point but to their credit, and the manager's, they stuck with it and even though they could only create half chances they did stay in the game. Amazingly, despite having taken their more illustrious opponents to a replay which was lost to a deflected goal, Batsford came under fire for not being aggressive in his tactics, but when you've equalled an FA Cup record with seven consecutive clean sheets and are known for having one of the meanest defences in the whole of non-league, it didn't worry the manager too much. As for Leeds, they did not retain the league title that season but did go on to the European Cup Final where they lost 2-0 to Bayern Munich.

The following season the Dons went on another run to FA Cup glory. This time they were afforded a late start as they entered the competition in the fourth qualifying round. A local derby against Kingstonian brought back some memories of clashes with the Ks through the decades, and Wimbledon, now in full flow, put their neighbours to the sword with a six-goal blast. Just over 3,000 came through the gate to see the Dons start their cup exploits with a goal inside ten minutes by Cooke, and although the visitors soon grabbed a goal back this only pushed

Wimbledon on harder. Bryant restored their lead before Mahon got another wonderful goal on the stroke of half-time. At 3-1 the game was all but done so Wimbledon played in a more relaxed manner and scored twice in a minute, Bryant with his second and Connell getting his obligatory goal. Edwards rounded the scoring off a couple of minutes from full time.

The first round brought some echoes of the past as the Dons were drawn against Nuneaton Borough, who had beaten them 2-0 to start the Batsford era. That game seemed a long time ago now, such was the amazing FA Cup run and then Southern League title win. Borough were on an unbeaten run of 18 games in the league, so came into this tie full of confidence, and backed by a crowd just shy of 4,500. Once more the game plan was set and Wimbledon shut down the Nuneaton attack and nicked the only goal at the start of the second half through Connell.

For the second round, Brentford were drawn out of the hat to visit Plough Lane. This was another one the Dons players and faithful could feel confident about. The Bees were a mid-table side in the Fourth Division, and with indifferent form. They had former Wimbledon goalkeeper Paul Priddy between the sticks, and whether that would play into their hands with inside knowledge only time would tell. Almost 8,400 packed into Plough Lane with lofty expectations but it was Brentford who struck first to quieten the crowd, then a second was added from the spot before half-time. Brentford shut up shop and got the win. The adventure would have to wait for at least one more year.

After a second successive Southern League championship there was ambitious talk of pushing for a promotion to the Football League but to do that, the Dons needed to put themselves back in front of the public. Winning non-league titles and trophies was one thing, but the Wimbledon board wanted more. Coming into the FA Cup first round weekend the Dons had lost three of their last four games ahead of a home tie against Isthmian League side Woking, who were making the short trip to Plough Lane. It was a special day for Dickie Guy, who was making his 500th first-team appearance. He did well to keep a clean sheet but was also thankful that striker Tony Roberts did not have his clean shooting boots on as he squandered two chances after the break with the game still tied 0-0. It wasn't until the 72nd minute that Wimbledon got the winner. A free kick from Bassett was flicked on by Holmes, with Bryant free to score.

More Isthmian League opponents were drawn out next, which meant another local team, as this time Leatherhead were the ones to try and knock the Dons off their perch. Wimbledon's form was still not great in the league and it was hoped that a cup run would be a spark. With a place in the third round on the line, and thoughts going back to the missed opportunity the season before, Wimbledon played with far more purpose, and despite some stubborn resistance early on the first goal was knocked in ten minutes before half-time, Bryant getting the breakthrough. Any chance of an upset was quelled just two minutes after the restart with Ricky Marlowe getting the first of his two goals, which were either side of a Reid effort for Leatherhead. Now the stage was set, with the third-round draw serving up another salivating tie.

Jack Charlton had won pretty much all there was to win – after all there is not much more to prove once you are a World Cup winner. But now he oversaw a Middlesbrough team struggling in the First Division. They wanted to make life as difficult as possible and unnerve the Dons, and part of the plan was a refusal to play under the floodlights so the kick-off was moved to a slightly earlier start of 2pm. A crowd of just over 8,500 was considered poor given the visitors for this tie and the push for promotion. Both teams blamed each other for not swelling the gate, or maybe it was the bad weather, a cold, dank day in south-west London, or it was possibly just good planning to stay away as the tie didn't live up to its pre-match hype. 'League teams never looked forward to playing us, they were used to their luxury,' said Dave Donaldson.

It was true; Plough Lane was the archetypal non-league ground with its muddy pitch, and low lighting, with dressing rooms that were small and pokey. A far cry from the Ayresome Park home comforts. That was the beauty of the FA Cup, though; the small teams had an advantage when they were paired up at home against a big club – it was the greatest of levellers. As well as Charlton being the manager, Middlesbrough had a certain Graeme Souness in their ranks at the start of his lengthy career. Wimbledon went toe-to-toe for most of the game, and chances were few and far between, but Donaldson also recalled a goal that was called back: 'We felt we had a perfectly good goal disallowed. Roger Connell put it in, and the referee harshly chalked it off. It would have been perfect justice for their arrogance.'

With the first game ending without a goal, it was up to Teesside for the replay three days later. Both sides were unchanged, but the one thing that had changed was the weather as a snow-covered pitch greeted the Dons. As with the Leeds game two years before the Wimbledon defence was holding firm and able to keep Boro at arm's length but the First Division side were relentless in their pursuit of a goal and eventually it came via a penalty. Kevin Tilley took down David Armstrong, who got up and placed the ball past Guy. It was tough on the young full-back who had a decent game, but as Armstrong got by him he had been late in the tackle. 'I just remember thinking it was so unnecessary. Yes, it was a penalty, but I thought there was no need for it, we should never have given it away,' said a despondent Ian Cooke, who had been helping cover the area as per the Batsford game plan. Every time a winger got the ball, the idea was to double up and with Cooke chaperoning Tilley they should have dealt with it better.

For Cooke it was bittersweet as it would be the last chance he would have at a giant-killing. Wimbledon would go on to win the Southern League again and duly get elected to the Football League. Cooke said, 'Allen had said that if we went into the league, we would stay part-time and that suited my career. But when it came to it the decision was taken to go full-time. I was 32 and that was when I left to join Slough.'

One of Wimbledon's best and most loyal servants would never get to play in the Football League. 'It was one of the biggest regrets of my life,' he added.

Two

The New Era

WITH ELECTION to the Football League, it was a
time of change at Plough Lane. Allen Batsford saw this
as the best time to step away; with chairman Ron Noades
tightening the purse strings it was difficult to make a
transition to league football as he would refuse to pay
expenses to the players so they could arrive at training.
It was just another thing that irked Batsford, and also in
his shadow was Dario Gradi, who Noades had brought
in to help with the running of the team. In January 1978
the Dons had just been beaten away by Swansea City.
'I just walked out,' Batsford said. 'I'd been placed in an
impossible position. Noades just didn't understand how to
run a football club. I still loved Wimbledon, but I felt that
Ron needed to leave before the club could progress again.
He wasn't going to, so I had to.'

Now in the Football League, Wimbledon no longer
had to navigate any qualifying rounds and had the

luxury of starting the FA Cup in the first round each year. This meant that the chance of being on the end of a giant-killing was less as the non-league teams were outnumbered by those playing alongside the Dons each week. That said, in the early years of this newfound success they did have their struggles. Indeed, in their first season as one of the bigger teams in the early rounds, and with Batsford still in charge, they were humbled 3-0 in front of nearly 3,000 at Enfield. It was a shock but Enfield, like Wimbledon had been, were a non-league big fish. This, though, was their first win against a team in the Football League.

In Gradi's first full season in charge he managed to get the team into the third round. Alan Cork netted a late winner in a replay against Gravesend, and then he rescued the Dons with a late equaliser in a replay at Bournemouth, before Steve Parsons scored directly from a corner. The third-round visitors to Plough Lane were First Division Southampton, and with them a bumper crowd of 9,254. A player who was already in FA Cup folklore, Charlie George, had recently signed for the Saints, but he was left out of the squad for this trip. Earlier in the season Wimbledon had travelled to Merseyside and got thumped 8-0 by Everton in the League Cup, with Bob Latchford bagging five. On this day it was Phil Bowyer who proved too hot as he grabbed a brace, but at 2-0 it was an improvement on the embarrassing reverse at Goodison.

After playing five games over two rounds in the following season's run, Wimbledon finally bowed out to a solitary goal in a second replay at home against Portsmouth. Middlesbrough awaited the winners, and on the back of a seven-game unbeaten run, confidence was high. An early goal settled the tie when Jeff Hemmerman beat the loose offside trap to score past Ray Goddard. Then in 1980/81, after smashing seven past Windsor & Eton in the first round, the Dons beat Swindon 2-0 and got past Oldham after a replay, Cork with yet another late show.

This set up a fourth-round tie in Wales as the faithful masses went to Wrexham. The Second Division side had beaten the holders West Ham United and were buoyant to the point that they held a 2-0 lead midway through the second half in this game. Paul Denny scored with just over 20 minutes to go to set up a great finish but the Dons couldn't score again, and exited the competition.

The consolation was that they only lost three more times that year as they gained promotion by finishing fourth. This was swiftly followed by relegation in 1982 under the stewardship of Dave Bassett in his first season at the helm. That season's FA Cup run was one to forget as after beating Bedford 2-0, they came up against Enfield again. They took an early lead and instead of capitalising on that, they sat back, invited the non-leaguers on and they had no hesitation in putting four into the Wimbledon net for another humiliation.

It wasn't much better in the 1982/83 FA Cup. The Bassett era had started poorly with relegation but there was no stopping Wimbledon as they roared to the Fourth Division title, losing only six games all season, amassing 98 points. The FA Cup run came to a swift end, however. After a battling fightback from two goals down, the Dons were helped by injuries and a red card for Northampton and had the chance to win the game in the last minute only for Chris Dibble to nod wide from mere yards out. In a severe rainstorm, the Cobblers didn't let Wimbledon off the hook in the replay, gaining an early advantage before sealing the game in the last minute.

Dave Bassett had the team playing free-flowing football and life in the Third Division was different this time around, scoring 97 goals as they finished second behind Oxford United to gain another promotion in 1983/84, and enter the second tier of English football for the first time. But just as in the season before, their FA Cup run was one to forget as following two goals from Cork to see off Orient, they lost a five-goal thriller at Brentford. It was a feisty game with 50 fouls committed between the two teams, and it was former Don Francis Joseph who got the Bees' third, and decisive goal, in an eventual 3-2 win. In the League Cup, Wimbledon beat former European Cup winners Nottingham Forest 3-1 over two legs, the highlight being a 2-0 win at Plough Lane. 'I don't think Forest really knew what to expect. They were flying in the

First Division, a huge club, up against little Wimbledon,' commented Steve Ketteridge. 'I remember everyone was doing their job, and doing it really well.'

The following season the two clubs would clash again, this time in the FA Cup, and the Forest team – with better preparation from Brian Clough – were ready, although if you can include a trip to Tenerife as part of the planning, it shows the gulf in extravagance. The problem was that this Forest team was a far cry from their European successes. They had come so far so quick under the excellent guidance of Clough that the fall was shockingly rapid, having been predicted to dominate as Liverpool had done in the 1970s. With an average start to the league season, and already out of the UEFA Cup in the first round, their last hope of silverware came with the domestic cups. They had also not been to the fourth round of the FA Cup for four years. Where a lot of the glory team had moved on Forest still had talent that, although not feared, could be revered. Steve Hodge was on the brink of being an England regular, and the Forest fans had yet to see the best of strike duo Garry Birtles and Peter Davenport. In goal was Dutchman Hans Segers, with defender Johnny Metgod known for his powerful shot. The match was played at the City Ground and the Dons' goal led a charmed life through the combination of Beasant and the woodwork, with the help of a couple of goal-line clearances. Clough now had to prepare his side for another trip down to little Plough Lane and its 'cosy' confines on a late January evening for a replay.

Over 10,000 were in attendance, producing record gate receipts. When the two sides met just a year earlier the Dons had shocked their opponents with their direct bruising style, but this time Forest were not to be overwhelmed. They played just as physically and made the game more interesting as a result. Just after ten minutes Paul Fishenden scored when his shot took a slight deflection off Kenny Swain and went in. Cue euphoria and the realisation that Wimbledon could actually humble the double European Cup winners of 1979 and 1980. Some hefty challenges went in for the remaining 80 minutes, and one from Steve Galliers caused Clough to lose his composure on the touchline. At the end of the game though he was magnanimous in defeat and knew that Wimbledon had once again outfought his side over the two games.

Wimbledon were in the fifth round, the last 16, for the first time. This was no fluke. It had been threatened for a while as the team was playing good attacking football under Dave Bassett, and mixing it with their no-nonsense style. It was a heady mix that rubbed some up the wrong way, but as anyone involved in team sports knows, you play to your strengths. That was exactly what Bassett was doing, and it was relentless. The draw had Wimbledon up against another top side, and the attractive playing style of West Ham would again prove a contrast to the neutral. In the build-up to the tie Wimbledon had beaten both Crystal Palace and Sheffield United 5-0. The two results ended a period of indifferent form in the league, and came at just the right time to put the Hammers more on their toes. The country was suffering from a severe cold snap, and the match, originally scheduled for 16 February, had been postponed twice which led to some fixture congestion. Having not won in the league in the calendar year, the east Londoners needed an FA Cup run to boost morale.

There's nothing like a good cup run and a local derby to get fans excited and once more Plough Lane was bursting for this Monday evening fixture under the floodlights, with 13,500 on the terraces and in the old stands. The game was a typical cup tie with lots of encouraging, fast play, and a few hard tackles. Alan Devonshire almost finished off a well-worked move on the right but had his tame, side-footed effort saved on the line by Dave Beasant. With just under 20 minutes left West Ham took the lead. Ray Stewart tried his luck from outside the area but it was going well wide, although instead it turned into a well-placed pass as it fell neatly into the path of Tony Cottee, who slipped the ball home. This left the Dons with nothing to lose and they threw everything forward. Nigel Winterburn was released down the left and his cross to Alan Cork saw the striker shoot high and wide. Wally Downes had come on for Glyn Hodges – the Welshman had earlier hit the post – and the substitution paid off. His deep cross found

Stewart Evans, whose glancing header went in off the far post for the equaliser.

The replay was just two days later, the third game in five days that both teams would play. Still over 20,000 piled into the Boleyn Ground, with a tasty quarter-final date at Old Trafford waiting for the winners the following Saturday. Wimbledon had not won on their travels since a New Year's Day victory at Oldham, and this game was one too many in the busy schedule. It would cause a hangover that saw three losses to the combined total of 11-1. Add in the 5-1 defeat at Upton Park and it was a desperate set of results.

West Ham were simply too good on the night, even after Fishenden had levelled Cottee's fifth-minute goal. Cottee would go on to complete a hat-trick while the Hammers' midfield were too classy and passed the ball around the Dons. It was a shame to go out in this manner, and Bassett's team would pick themselves up to finish a respectable 12th in the league. 'We didn't deserve to finish so heavily punished. But we can still go out with our heads held high and the knowledge we travelled further and made more money than any Wimbledon side previously,' said Bassett in his programme notes in the next home match. 'Two hectic games in such a short period was just too much for even seasoned professional. I'm not saying we shouldn't have been forced through the tortuous 72 hours, but once again, it underlines how a rich club, with their undersoil heating, can hope and further prosper over the not so wealthy.'

Wimbledon knew though that after the past two seasons they were on the brink of something special and despite a third-round defeat at Millwall the next year, they would go on to achieve another promotion, their third in four seasons. This took them to the First Division. All that had gone on before, the long FA Cup runs in the 1970s, the heroes made along the way, had been remarkable enough. Now, though, they were truly in dreamland.

Having made their name in the FA Cup, Wimbledon were not going to rest on that alone. Now they had a point to prove that they were more than a flash in the pan, more than a kick-and-rush team. Although those tactics remained, why change something if it's working? After an opening-day loss at Manchester City to kick off the 1986/87 season, a three-goal blast in six minutes cancelling out an Andy Thorn goal, they went on a four-game winning run that took the Dons to the top of the league. Wimbledon were at the very summit of English football. We could stop there and declare the story over – it surely couldn't get any better than that.

That first year at the top meant the Dons were mixing it with the big boys on a weekly basis, and along with their exploits in years gone by, the ability to put a cup run together was part of the club's DNA. By the time the third round of the FA Cup came along they were sitting comfortably in the middle of the table, having just beaten West Ham and Watford over a busy Christmas.

Sunderland, from the Second Division, were a potential banana skin to slip on if the Dons weren't at their best. Their team was made up of hardy veteran players like George Burley, Eric Gates and Alan Kennedy, and they had the potential to keep things tight. Manager Lawrie McMenemy, no stranger to winning trophies himself, watched as Gates was given time and space to shoot past a stranded Beasant. It looked like it was another wasted opportunity, but Lawrie Sanchez, always one to pop up with a vital goal, did just that, turning in a loose ball following a Hodges corner. 'As we were coming off at half-time, he [Gates] was giving it large,' Hodges said, 'saying we were this and that and weren't worthy of being in the First Division.' Sometimes team talks aren't needed, as these words stung and motivated the Dons. Then in the last minute provider turned into scorer as Hodges escaped the tiring Sunderland defence to seal a dramatic late turnaround. 'We eventually won by reaching deep into reserves, with two goals in the last two minutes. But it was the other 88 that worried me. Many of the team I've noticed are seemingly content with what they've achieved, settling for mid-table thinking, and possibly pulling out the extra for the cup. That is not, and will never be, Wimbledon thinking,' noted Bassett.

After a stern talking-to the Dons had the luxury of a mini break away in the Algarve to reset and come back ready for the next round against Portsmouth. Again, the draw was kind, putting Bassett's team at home, and with a chance to progress to the fifth round for only the second time it was one that they didn't let go.

Second Division leaders Pompey were managed by Alan Ball, who was no stranger to big games and winning significant trophies, but he was in total disbelief at the horror show his team served up in the first half. The World Cup winner may have wished he could have laced up his boots again, but at 3-0 down even he knew it was all over, and when the Dons added a fourth it was back to the south coast with their tails between their legs. John Fashanu got the first goal after Alan Knight failed to clear his lines, then an own goal was followed by an Andy Sayer strike. Fashanu got his second with half an hour left.

Then came the big one. The stage was set on a blustery afternoon and the visit of top-of-the-table Everton would be shown live on the BBC. Having television cameras around was not new – local stations had been covering Wimbledon for many years, and the recent success had seen national crews come and cover games on highlight shows, or big feature spots. This, though, was a new ball game. Everton were the business, a slick football machine that knew how to handle big-game pressure. They had reached the last three FA Cup finals, beating Watford 2-0 in 1984, losing 1-0 to Manchester United the following year, and then in the first all-Merseyside final they were defeated

3-1 by their red rivals. Now, their team full of international stars were back at Plough Lane after winning 2-1 there in the early part of the season and completing the double with a 3-0 victory at Goodison Park just before Christmas.

Trevor Steven, who always made the game look easy, found some rare space in a fiercely contested midfield and played a ball to the right for Adrian Heath to attack. Beasant came out to try and slow the move down, but Heath danced around him and from the byline arced a cross over where Wilkinson nodded home from virtually on the goal line. With a fourth-minute lead it seemed like the Toffees had taken the wind out of the Dons' sails. It took them a while to get into the game and chances were hard to come by, until a minute before the half-time whistle. Fashanu ran for about 20 yards with full-back Gary Stevens all over him, pulling and tugging until in the end, with the pair just inside the box, the contact was too much and the big striker went down. Andy Sayer took the spot kick and although Neville Southall guessed correctly, diving to his right to parry the attempt away, three Dons were rushing in fast. Hodges was first to the ball and gleefully slammed it in the net. Honours even at half-time, but a late goal always puts the scorers in the ascendency.

John Motson was commentating in a temporary gantry on top of the South Stand, alongside Bobby Robson. They both recognised the fact that Wimbledon were not there just to make up the numbers, and when a huge kick from

Beasant was flicked on to Sayer on the left of the Everton area another goal looked possible. Southall got down quickly to save the shot but the ball ran out to Fashanu just inside the box. After a smart touch to get the ball out of his feet and a quick check of his surroundings he drilled the ball into the net. The commentators were right, and the Dons were ahead with half an hour to play.

The clock was starting to go slower now with fans checking their watches, every minute seeming like five. With 15 left Sayer got his goal, his tenacity paying off. Another long punt from Beasant saw the ball practically on the edge of the Everton box, and from there Sayer did the rest as he got a break away from his marker after a Fashanu flick-on. He jinked to the right around Kevin Ratcliffe and let loose a shot that went under Southall for 3-1 and sparked delirium on the terraces. Sayer later recalled, 'It was one of those special days when you could really sense the Wimbledon spirit.'

Was this finally the coming-of-age story, the day that Wimbledon not only made believers of those who doubted their status, but also of their peers and equals on the football pitch? Everton manager Howard Wilkinson told local reporters, 'In all our previous matches against Wimbledon, and teams in a similar mould, we have managed to compete with them physically. On this occasion we didn't. When they were on the attack, it wasn't so much their first ball that caused us problems, but the second ball. In other words, while we coped quite well with their long forward passes into our box, they reacted quicker than us when the ball broke loose. Full credit to Wimbledon, they are a team who never accept defeat.'

Tottenham Hotspur manager David Pleat went on record to say that Wimbledon were no longer a fairy tale, they had become a reality. Later, on *Match of the Day*, Don Howe mused with Bob Wilson about the long-ball game, but as Howe rightly pointed out goals like the third had been scored since football had started and it was up to teams to combat it.

Neville Southall, one of the best players in Europe at the time and as Everton's goalkeeper the last line of their defence against Wimbledon, said, 'I found as a club they had a "we don't give a shit who you are" attitude, always the underdog, but it masked a team full of quality. A great blend of determination, fighting spirit and fun. I loved playing against them, but if you were not ready for the physical battle first you would lose. They did the things they were good at very well and put immense effort into things they were not good at. Character in abundance, always well organised, and I loved the way they tried to intimidate teams. I found it fun.'

Just as *Match of the Day* had covered the previous round, no one wanted to miss the story of the quarter-finals, so *The Big Match*'s outside broadcast units arrived with their personalities Ian St John and Jimmy Greaves, and the commentator Brian Moore. It was unthinkable to many, or at least those outside of the Wimbledon bubble, that this team had risen so quickly. Dave Bassett was doing his best to keep everyone's feet on the ground, which was a far from easy task, so he took the players away again for a few days in the sun. The golf may have had something to do with it, but the team needed to stay focused and doing that without any home distractions was considered the best way.

Opponents Tottenham Hotspur were the Rolls-Royce of football. They often purred when they played, through the influence of Glenn Hoddle, who was considered one of the best players in Europe, let alone the English game. This was on top of a side that had Ray Clemence in goal, Gary Stevens, Richard Gough and Gary Mabbutt marshalling the defence, Chris Waddle with his lazy runs, and Paul and Clive Allen finishing things off up front. On paper, just as Everton before, the Dons looked outmatched. But as Howard Kendall said after he saw his team beaten, 'With their immense physical power, they will create as many problems for Tottenham as they did for us.'

The game was again played in windy conditions, with over 15,500 packed in. It was a cracking atmosphere and more tense than against Everton. This could have been because of the prize at stake, or the fact it was a London team that were buying their way to potential glory. In the main it was an untidy tie which was separated by two moments of magic, although unfortunately they came from the team all in white. Seven minutes from the end Waddle played a short one-two with Nico Claesen, and as he slowed outside the box to see his options, the Belgian decided to take on the last man, Winterburn. For the first time he managed to get around the outside of the full-back and instead of shooting he angled a cross in before he ran out of play. The ball arrowed in, and the Wandle End of the ground erupted. Waddle sunk to his knees halfway through his celebration, due to relief and tiredness. Wimbledon were known for their late shows, but this now seemed beyond even them, and when Hoddle lined up a free kick fully 30 yards from goal after Andy Thorn had hacked Waddle down, there was only one thing on his mind. He struck the ball so well it was up and over Beasant before his outstretched arm was fully extended.

'I know we could have done much better, and certainly forced a draw. But at the end of the day, we didn't do what we are usually good at – score. I also blame myself for the defeat. I asked several players to move into roles they weren't familiar with, and it didn't work. It was my mistake entirely,' said Bassett when summing up the quarter-final in his next programme notes.

Wimbledon would finish in sixth place in their first journey through England's elite, winning 19 games from the 42 played, losing 14. Everton went on to win the First Division, ahead of Liverpool, with Tottenham in third, just five points ahead of the Dons. The FA Cup run, with its two nationally televised games, meant that just as those of the 1975 team, the names of Fashanu, Sayer, Hodges, Beasant and Dave 'Harry' Bassett were known across the land.

This was just the beginning.

The Defender's Story
Clive Goodyear

CLIVE GOODYEAR moved south from his Lincoln home and found himself a regular in the Luton Town first team after making his debut aged 17. After a handful of years there and almost 100 appearances, he moved further south, and a bit west, when he landed at Plymouth Argyle. So how did this studious professional end up at Wimbledon in 1987? 'My contract was up at the end of my third year at Argyle, and we just missed out on getting into the play-offs to get into the First Division. And in my mind, at that point the club just wasn't ambitious enough. I was looking for a move, and oddly enough I'd agreed to go to York City, which would have been big given there wasn't even an M25 back then! Then, at the last minute I had a call from Bobby Gould at Wimbledon saying they were interested in signing me. So that's how it came about. I ended up meeting him down at the Robin Hood training ground and went from there. It was another chance to get back playing in the First Division at the time.'

It was a summer of change in SW19, with new manager Bobby Gould making moves in the transfer market and getting new defenders in over the summer. Goodyear continued, 'There was a lot of us signing at the same time, [John] Scales, [Eric] Young, [Terry] Phelan, so we were all battling for a place to start. I missed the very first game as I got a little hip injury when we were on a pre-season tour of Sweden, so I missed the game at Watford. I was on the bench for the Derby County game, which was my debut when I came on as sub, and then I got injured.' Goodyear had been lucky with injuries up to then in his career, but then had a series of them that would eventually cut his time short at the club, 'It was one of those years. I'd gone ten years without anything, then the year I signed at Wimbledon I had three quite major ones really. An ankle ligament, and a small fracture in my left fibula kept me out for six weeks or so after that game with Derby.'

The back line was ever changing through suspensions and injuries but Goodyear, when available, was always favoured. So much so that he was in all the games in the FA Cup run, except one. 'A fracture below the kneecap – out of the semi-final – it was against my old team as well. It would have been nice to have played in that one. It was not an enjoyable afternoon, until the end. Sitting and watching, I'd rather have been playing. I had about four or five weeks until the final after the semi. So I went up to Lilleshall for three weeks, to the rehabilitation centre there, getting healed and fit to come back, and have a chance of playing. Because it was a bone injury the time would be for that to heal, that was the real race against time. The healing process, everything else would have been OK. Once I got the go-ahead to start getting involved in proper training, I was very hopeful again.'

The time away was fruitful in the end, but it meant missing out on some of the FA Cup Final razzmatazz. 'I missed out on a lot of the build-up as I was at Lilleshall for those three weeks. So I did miss what was going on at the training ground, I was back home at weekends for the games, but missed all the other shenanigans, making the record and that sort of thing, but I was totally focused on getting fit and giving myself every chance of getting in the team and playing.' Goodyear did get back and was in the team before the end of the season, playing against Norwich City and Manchester

United, then came the call-up for the final, 'It was a surprise. I was always hoping. I'd give it my all in training and in the games, but it was a very pleasant surprise to be honest.'

It was now a case of making the most of it and on the eve of the big game, some tension had to be released. 'From my point of view we were all a bit restless and couldn't settle down properly. So Bobby gave Dave [Beasant] some money and said go down to the pub and relax. Have a couple of drinks and come back up. Until that point, I'd never had a drink the night before a game. I ended having five or six pints of Guinness! But it did help me sleep, I have to say. As for anything else that happened, I'm not sure if it was made up by the press, but nothing out of order happened as far as I know. It was just a few drinks to relax us, and it did the trick.'

The team were used to being on television now, in various forms, but they had not been chosen for a live game so far in 1987/88, so was it unusual when all of a sudden, on the morning of the final, cameras were everywhere and broadcasting live to the nation? 'The TV cameras didn't put us off, I think we all enjoyed the occasion of it all. As a little boy growing up you always watch the cup final from nine or ten in the morning, all day, that's what I always wanted to be part of, so as far as I was concerned it was great.' And the journey from the hotel just added to it all, said Goodyear: 'Anticipation. Excitement. And just a mass of red. Driving up Wembley Way it all seemed to be Liverpool fans. But it was good nerves, and that's what you want it to be.' It was one of the hottest days of the year, if not the hottest, and stepping out in their suits the players, and Clive, finally got to live their dream out in reality. 'It was very warm, yes, and it's what you've watched over the years and wanted to be part of. Just walking out, and taking it all in. I think because I was late being called into the team coming back from the injury, I was determined to take it all in and enjoy it more because I nearly didn't play. I really did enjoy every moment of it.'

Then it was down to business, and the last team talk before the biggest game of their careers. Goodyear recalled what they had been told, 'Play our game, don't get drawn into doing anything different to what we'd planned and worked on. If we all did our jobs as talked about, we'd give Liverpool a game, and have a chance. It was just about being ourselves as we had done all season so why change? It was just a reminder of what each individual's job was in the game, pretty simple really. We finished seventh in the league, with a not-so-great run at the end of the season, so we really did believe we had a chance on the day if we did our jobs and stuck to the plan.'

The goal, coming after a let-off when Peter Beardsley had one disallowed, gave further belief. 'It came ten minutes before half-time or thereabouts, so it was good going into half-time with a lead and it gave us something to play for.'

For the most part the plan was stuck to, but some things you can't account for, so when Goodyear was adjudged to have given away a penalty it was a definite shock: 'I got into a good position. I read the pass coming through, and managed to slide and play the ball back to Dave, so when the whistle went it was hard to take in. I could not believe it. I don't think I even made contact with [John] Aldridge, he just fell over my legs, so it was upsetting to say the least. It was quite a shock that the penalty was given.'

After Beasant had made his historic save, however, Goodyear had different feelings, 'I had massive relief at that moment. I thought this could be our day as he saved it. It went right for us. Then the corner comes over and he drops it and had to dive on it again! But at that moment I thought this could definitely be our day.' The clock started to slow down after that. 'I think speaking to my family it was longer for them, but it was a good test of my personal fitness at that time, because in that heat it was quite hard in the end. I'm just pleased it didn't go into extra time. I suppose the last five minutes did drag on a little bit as we were getting so close, but again the whole team was great in the concentration of the jobs we were there for, and we came through it. Over the years watching finals, you know when the stewards and constables come out, you noticed that was happening so I knew the end wasn't far away.'

Referee Brian Hill blew the final whistle, leaving Goodyear delighted, 'Just pure relief and joy really, a dream come true. It was one of the longest laps of honour ever I think, we seemed to walk around forever. [In the changing room] I think just everybody sat down and took a while to take it in really and reflect on it – it was quiet, and then after ten minutes or so everybody just started celebrating and enjoying the moment.' The prearranged celebration back at Plough Lane and the day after will live long in the memory too. 'We all had our families there and it was a great evening. My family got all the papers the next morning back home, and everyone was reading them when we went down for breakfast. Once we got up the road into town, and saw all the fans appear from nowhere, it was far more than we anticipated really, some say the numbers were around 25,000.'

The team couldn't repeat the success the following season, but Goodyear didn't even get as far as the showpiece opener at Wembley. 'I got injured a week before the Charity Shield. It was a more serious injury which led to me being out for a year. We were banned from Europe so couldn't play in the Cup Winners' Cup which was a shame really as I'd love to have seen us marauding around Europe. It's a shame we didn't stay together for longer to see where we could have gone but that's football. I spent most of that season watching because of the knee injury. I played another handful of games, but it was a cruciate knee injury, and I just couldn't play at that level again, it wasn't right.'

Reflecting in general on that season, it was hard not to smile about it for Goodyear, 'Going into that Crazy Gang environment was a great experience, I loved every minute of it. It was a laugh every day, training was always enjoyable, everything we did as a group was enjoyable, except for me personally with the injury at the end of that first year. A great experience.'

Three

The Transition

'I LOVED my time at Wimbledon. I remember the characters among the fans as much as the players. Nelsons nightclub, where the fans and the players would mix. It was unique. There was a feeling at Wimbledon that everyone was in it together.'

After 13 years as a player, assistant manager and manager, Dave 'Harry' Bassett was leaving the club. He had been one of the few who had seen it all, from Southern League titles and taking on league champions Leeds United as part of an epic FA Cup run to taking the Dons to sixth place in the First Division. It had truly been an amazing period, one which will live long in the memories of those who were fortunate to be part of it all. As Bassett said, everyone was in it together. The fans took to the players as family. It was a well-worn cliche that Wimbledon was a family club, and you only realise it when you are involved and have it as part of your routine. The nightclub did serve its purpose to bring that to the fore. Score a winner and you would celebrate with the fans. Have a bad night and you would soon forget it as the fans would pick you up.

Like any club from humble non-league surroundings, it was hard to shake that background off when you found success. The thing was that with Wimbledon the success was so fast they outgrew themselves; the ground just couldn't adapt around the club as it raced through the leagues. This had its merits as the likes of Brian Clough, Howard Kendall and Alex Ferguson would testify. Bassett may have respected the opposition, but he didn't fear them, and this rubbed off on his teams. You didn't get to where the club was by luck – it was hard work, really hard work.

As with all good things though, they come to an end. The end had nearly come sooner as Bassett had a brief flirtation with Crystal Palace when he quit the Dons shortly after gaining promotion to the Second Division, but after just three days he came back. This may have been the beginning of the end though as owner Sam Hammam, although enjoying the progression of the club on the field, didn't want anyone other than himself getting the full limelight for its achievements. Bassett said, 'My contract was up [at the end of the 1986/87 season] and I felt Sam wanted me to go.' Hammam may have wanted that but the fans voiced their support as the season drew to a finish.

The last four games were won as Wimbledon climbed up to sixth. It was a fitting conclusion to an amazing first season at the top table; the last home game ended with the customary civil pitch invasion and the home crowd singing their 'Don't go, Harry!' plea on repeat. The same thing happened again on the final day of the long campaign away at Sheffield Wednesday. The fans knew what was happening but how else could they say goodbye as a collective than actually asking for Bassett not to go as a sign of appreciation?

This was a major turning point for the club. With the man who had led the team departing, some of the players would follow. Watford was the destination of choice. After Graham Taylor had been tempted away by Aston Villa, it was said that Wimbledon were the new Watford, so the switch made tactical sense for Bassett and those he took to Vicarage Road. Bassett was able to convince two players to join him, defender Mark Morris, and winger Glyn Hodges. 'Dave called me and said, "You fancy coming to Watford?" At the time it seemed a good career move,' Morris said, the defender having played over 20 times in the last season. Hodges had a 'what if?' moment after he left the Dons, later admitting, 'I honestly believe that side could have won a number of trophies if we had stayed together.'

Also leaving were Kevin Gage and Nigel Winterburn, both hugely influential over the past few season, with Winterburn being a firm fan favourite. Gage had joined as an apprentice in 1980 and played a pivotal role in the rise of the club, 'I played every minute of every game that season [51 in total in 1986/87], so it was personally quite an achievement. I knew Bassett was leaving at the end of the season. We all did. I also knew Hodges, Morris and Nigel were out of contract and would probably be going too, along with some others in the squad. I had always signed one-year contracts, so I was out of contract too. I personally felt that I'd achieved just about everything I could at Wimbledon having joined them in the old Fourth Division, and just thought that it was time my career moved on too.'

Gage retained many fond memories about his final season at Plough Lane, including this particular one from Old Trafford. 'The game was uneventful, a run-of-the-mill 1-0 win for us. I was up against Gordon Strachan, who gave me little trouble all afternoon. I was booked in the second half for "elbowing" him in the head, as we both went up for the ball, but as he's only about 5ft 5in tall, its easily done and there was genuinely no malice in it. So, game over, and I'm in the busy players' bar, making my way past some people seated at tables carrying three pints pressed together in my hands, as you do.

'Arms are splayed out a bit to ensure balance, and I accidentally knock an elbow into a lady's head. No harm done, I apologise and move on, pints duly delivered. I realise after about ten minutes, and because of the two ginger-haired kids running around her, that the lady was Mrs Strachan. So, I'd elbowed both Strachans at this stage! Another 15 minutes or so and I'm again making my way from the bar with some drinks when lo and behold one of the Strachan kids now runs into me! I got a glimpse of him charging along not looking where he was going and so kind of braced myself, but he ran into my arm/elbow anyway. So that's three of the Strachan family down, one to go. It caused a great deal of hilarity on our players' table anyway.

'A few pints later and it's time to leave. The Strachan kids are now playing football in the corridor just outside the players' bar and we are walking towards them. I'm currently three and one with the family so can't resist the opportunity to get involved, dribble the ball up to the remaining and youngest Strachan, tempt him towards me and very gently deliver an elbow to the head. The poor kid just stared at me wondering what the hell I was doing as I walked away giggling to myself. It wasn't big and it wasn't clever but sometimes opportunity knocks, and things just have to be done. It's kept me amused for all these years and I always still smile when I see the fella on TV!'

There's no doubt that the great team ethic helped Wimbledon achieve success, but certain individuals stood out from the others. Winterburn was destined for Arsenal as word got out of his contract being up, but he recalled his origin story with the Dons, 'I was without a club so had to make sure my month-long trial finished with an offer of a contract.' Bassett had come calling after an original approach for Brian Sparrow of Arsenal fell through.

Winterburn continued, 'I remember Dave telling me that to start with he did not want to play me in the first pre-season friendlies as I was very quiet, then in one of the games we got an injury and he put me on. He decided after that game that he would sign me.' The full-back didn't look back after that and was voted fans' player of the season for four consecutive years. In 1986/87 he was ever present, 'It was such an amazing time for me with the supporters voting for me in each of those seasons which ended with the [eventual] transfer to Arsenal. We used to ask in the office what scouts were watching the home games each week and if the big clubs were there it added extra incentive. As soon as Arsenal had the offer accepted and I went for talks with George Graham I knew I would sign for them.'

With the unthinkable now a reality, it was a time of transition at the club with players leaving, and others perhaps unsure of where they stood in terms of a new manager coming in. The boots of Dave Bassett were big ones to fill. It wasn't just the continuation of the spirit that was needed, it was an escalation of it. Having come so far, to have any standards stagnate or slip just wouldn't be the Wimbledon way, but as far as anyone could see there was no one else like 'Harry' so a replacement was likely to ring the changes. Then again, anyone on the outside looking in would be foolish to tamper with a team that was so unorthodox but had gained such a remarkable set of results and promotions. Wimbledon were riding the waves, and all that it needed was a steady hand on the rudder to keep the ship going straight.

As with any managerial job, a shortlist was drawn up of possible replacements, and one name was starting to rise to the top, especially as he had made it known that he would like to be considered for the vacant position. His football credentials were very smart and he was a name that most would recognise. He had previously managed in the top division only once, an 18-month stint in charge of Coventry City, but his playing career was where he had made his name, scoring 160 goals in 440 appearances. 'When the phone rang, I was away on holiday with the family in Corfu,' Bobby Gould recalled. 'It was Stanley Reed.' The Dons' chairman asked Gould quite simply if he would be interested in the job. 'I told him I was extremely interested,' Gould said. This was the start of a great relationship, and when he met Reed, and Sam Hammam, everything fell into place. The decision wasn't taken lightly to leave Bristol Rovers, his current employers, a team playing within its means but holding its own in the Third Division. As well as being part of the fabric at Rovers, Gould would have to move his family again, and this was a crucial time of his sons' schooling, all things to consider when taking on a new job. 'If it hadn't been a top-flight club, I wouldn't have gone,' he admitted.

Ever the professional, the adjustment came quite easily for Gould, even if the immediate day-to-day change wasn't straightforward. Taking over the headlined 'Crazy Gang' was not going to be an easy task, unless you had that streak in you too and could fall in line with the playground antics and bring your own ammunition to the parade. As a precursor, Gould had already had a short spell with the club and knew what to expect from that, and also knowing what everyone else saw and read each week. Back in 1981, at the tail end of his playing career, the striker still had some gas left in the tank to burn off. Keeping a close eye on clubs that needed help he noticed that Dave Bassett was on the lookout for 'experienced' forwards. It was perfect. After giving Bassett a call and telling him he had someone in mind for his job search, the laughter still rings in Gould's ears when he told the manager it was himself. Nonetheless, he was told to report for training in pre-season. If nothing else it would keep him sharp for any other opportunity.

Back off his holidays and bronzed, he fell victim to the first of the group's jokes when they gave him the moniker 'Moroccan Mole', but this was perhaps a double meaning as they weren't taking his try-out seriously and thought this was an underhand tactic by Bassett, who they believed had installed Gould as a spy. This was the summer after winning promotion to the Second Division, and Gould was taking his training seriously, and after tripling his weekly wage from £20 to £60 he was dead set on making this work.

Sam Hammam was impressed with the work ethic of the veteran player, and after a pre-season friendly and some run-outs in the reserves, it looked like Gould would actually get into the first team to start the season as Alan Cork had unfortunately broken his leg. Then on the eve of the campaign he got a call from Aldershot. The offer they gave him to become player-coach just couldn't be matched; Wimbledon's wage bill could not stretch that far. Gould wanted to stay having earned the players' respect and proved himself capable. He went to Bassett and as a compromise for giving him the chance, offered to stay for £80 a week, half of what the Shots had put on the table. It wasn't to be though and the brief flirtation with the Dons ended, although Hammam had not forgotten by the time his 1987 interview for the manager's job came around. As part of the deal to bring Gould on board he had to have a property near the ground, and as a short-term fix, Hammam helped the new gaffer by letting him stay in his flat. It wasn't long though before he found his own place and was able to get to work each day with just a short walk.

The very humble training ground at the Richardson Evans playing fields was still non-league in its setup. The manager's office was set at the back of a transport cafe, and to get there it wouldn't be too uncommon to have rubbed shoulders with taxi drivers, or other workers either at the end of their shift, or just starting. This was all part of the charm though, a real sense of being among the working people in life, and it helped keep everyone's feet firmly on the ground. Gould, through his very brief time at Wimbledon just a few years before, saw a few familiar faces as he settled in, and even some of the same players were still there. This was, after all, when being a one-club man wasn't too far a stretch, and freedom of contract wasn't even a pipe dream. The newer breed of players had taken the Dons past that next step, and to do so had to be big and brash to survive the daily onslaught of training-ground terrors that other players would enforce. The likes of John Fashanu, Vinnie Jones and Dennis Wise proved to be the catalyst of the team spirit. With Lawrie Sanchez, Andy Thorn and Carlton Fairweather creating the core of the squad, it was easy to see why the Wimbledon team of the mid-1980s had done so well. They were footballers first and pranksters second, although they would have you believe otherwise.

However, there were certain pieces missing that needed addressing before anything else, including the not-so-small matter of the backroom staff. As good as Gould and his current set of players were, they couldn't do the job without a set of staff that would be up to the task of taking on, and beating, some of Europe's best teams. The bar had been set very high by Bassett and his group, who he took with him when leaving for Watford, and only the best would do for Gould. For his first appointment he took a step back in time to call upon the services of Ron Stuart. The two had worked together at Chelsea when World Cup-winning hero Geoff Hurst was in charge of the Blues, although Gould had as much say in the running of the team as Hurst did, and at that time both were a little out of their depth even as Chelsea struggled and were swimming in debt. The first piece of the puzzle was Stuart, a loyal man and one who Gould could trust without having to look over his shoulder.

When forming his staff it was important to be open to new ideas, a fresh set of eyes, someone to see things that you couldn't, even if they were right in front of you. Don Howe had pretty much done everything in terms of playing and coaching. After almost 350 appearances for West Bromwich Albion in the 1950s and early '60s he moved south to end his playing career at Arsenal. Starting his managerial career, he went back to the Baggies for the first half of the 1970s, and his last role as the top man in the dugout was back at Arsenal until he resigned towards the end of the 1985/86 season. As a coach he also had stints at Leeds and Galatasaray, and also helped Ron Greenwood at the 1982 World Cup as the England team went unbeaten but fell short in the second group phase. When it came to coaching in the English game, there really was no one more qualified who happened to be free. The trouble was, would a club like Wimbledon be suited to the more 'classic' style of football that Howe's teams played? There was only one way to find out.

Gould had worked with Howe before during his days at Arsenal, and clearly knew his depth of knowledge would be perfect, and if he could bring an ounce of respect and order to the dressing room with him then that would be a bonus. After a call and some time explaining the situation, it was agreed that Howe would come along for a month and see how things went. This was a major coup. All Gould needed was to show him that this team weren't just the long-ball merchants that everyone perceived them to be, and he would have a great ally in building for the future.

Recruitment continued and in need of a decent physiotherapist, Gould tapped up the Football Association to see who the brightest young person in this area was. This led him to Steve Allen, who at just 21 years old could and would gel with the players and be one of them as well as their healer. Inheriting the popular sports masseuse Caroline Brouwer, and kit man Syd Neal, he also had Dave Kemp to look after the reserves. 'I was very pleased to get the job and I'll be making the most of it. I love coaching and I'm really enjoying working with the youngsters,' Kemp said of his appointment. Howe recommended the services of Terry Burton, who was at Arsenal, to look after the fine talent in the youth system. It was all coming together nicely, and now it was just a case of finding the players to replace those who had followed Bassett off to Watford or had gone elsewhere to continue their footballing dreams.

Four

Laying Foundations

THE REBUILDING phase started as soon as Bobby Gould knew he had the job. His contacts book was big, but the Dons' budget was not. With his staff assembled it was a time to quickly assess and address what the needs were, and the biggest holes created by players leaving the club. Depth of squad was essential too, but with the Wimbledon youth system one of the best in London they had players coming up who could be tested if necessary. Perhaps the biggest chasm to fill was that of Nigel Winterburn, with the full-back lured away to north London, and the marble halls of Highbury. The attacking play of Glyn Hodges, and the versatility of Mark Morris, Kevin Gage and John Kay would need to be replaced too, but it would also be a time when current squad players would be able to make their mark.

John Scales was the first major signing of the summer, costing £75,000. Scales, at 21, was a young talent who

Gould had at Bristol Rovers and had previously been on the books at Leeds United. He was a versatile defender, and his adaptive qualities would be an asset, even if he was a little unassuming when he first came through the door. 'The move was a bit of a shock for me,' the converted striker said upon signing. 'There has been a fantastic success story here. We are now all determined to prove that it is not a one-off. I'm looking forward to playing a higher standard of football and improving my game.'

A new back line was going to be paraded on the opening day of the season if the new players coming in were anything to go by. Filling the full-back role was Terry Phelan. The left-sided player was a year younger than Scales but had already been honoured at international level, having picked up a youth appearance for the Republic of Ireland. His was quick, very quick, and this was one attribute that had led to him being named in the Professional Footballers' Association Team of the Year while playing for Swansea City. The £90,000 fee was seen as a bargain. The slight figure of Phelan had first been at Leeds United, Billy Bremner letting him go on a free to the Welsh club, but after a full season at the Vetch Field it was money well spent in the eyes of Gould. Again, though, he was a quiet lad, and just wanted to get on with his football. Getting used to the training-ground antics was something that would take time.

Another defensive position was filled with the arrival of Clive Goodyear. His experience was something that would come in handy alongside the younger players who were coming in. Goodyear had played his part in Luton Town's early time in the First Division under the stewardship of David Pleat. He played close to 100 games for the Hatters before moving on to Plymouth Argyle in 1984, where he went on to go beyond the century mark. The signing, for £50,000, was shrewd business.

The last part of the defensive jigsaw was in place when £60,000 was handed over for the towering centre-back Eric Young. If the club staff thought the new players were quiet, then Young would turn out to be something of a recluse. A trio of seasons at non-league Slough Town kicked off his career, before Brighton & Hove Albion acquired him for £10,000, where he went on to play in excess of 120 games over four seasons for the Sussex coast team. Along with 20-year-old Andy Thorn, and Brian Gayle who was just 22, the back line had a youthful look to it, but they had lots of league games under their belts. Thorn had just come back from a successful youth tournament in France where he earned the accolade of best defender among the competing teams, which included the Ivory Coast national side.

For top teams, pre-season tours were now starting to be commonplace. Scandinavia often proved to be the choice for the Dons and so as part of preparation for the long season ahead, and also part of the team bonding, the staff and players packed their bags and headed for Sweden. The chosen opposition was of poor standard, and in the five games played Wimbledon outscored their opponents by a combined 25-1, with Alan Cork and John Fashanu netting six times each, Fash scoring in each game. Something that Gould wanted his players to know was that they weren't small-time any more, and when the team first arrived they were put up in a small motel. This was in keeping with the Crazy Gang attitudes, but hardly good for match preparation.

Together, Gould and Don Howe agreed that they needed an upgrade, and after some quick discussions with the tour organiser at the club they moved to a more suitable hotel: four stars, no less. The first meeting of all the new staff was one that changed the landscape of how the two would manage the squad going forward. Armed with a flip chart and pen, Howe was busy presenting his tactics. It was standard stuff but this team was far from being standard. The icebreaker was when the leaders of the pack got up and said their piece. Fash, Vinnie, Sanchez, Beasant and Cork took centre stage. Perplexed but not put out, Howe stepped aside and let them talk. It was telling them, and reminding themselves of who they were, and what they were all about, and how training would go down. Even to the precise amount of set pieces they would practise, 44 to be exact. Yes, they could take on new ideas, but the Wimbledon Way wouldn't change. Getting the ball up the pitch and into the opponents' area via long, direct passing had got them this far so why change it.

Gould recalled the days he spent trying to keep his playing career going, and those weeks under Dave Bassett when he would say near enough the same thing as he was being told now. Instead of telling them to sit down and shut up, Gould let the players continue to an end. He was pleased to have so many leaders in his dressing room. He would have to keep them ticking over, but knowing that this team would fight for each other, just as much as they would pull pranks, it would save him a rallying cry or two.

Arriving back from Sweden, the Dons were straight off the plane to play Reading at Elm Park. It was clear to see that the trip and travel had taken their toll as the team laboured to a 1-0 win, with Fashanu keeping up his scoring run, a fine finish just before the hour. Former Don Francis Joseph came closest to scoring for the home side with a low drive that Dave Beasant was equal to. A couple of days later a much-changed side lost 4-2 at Maidstone, the part-timers running up the result despite Carlton Fairweather opening the scoring. The final pre-season outing was the trip to Cambridge United, who had caused an upset against the Dons in the previous season's League Cup, now sponsored by Littlewoods. The Fourth Division side beat the Dons again, 2-1, and even felt generous enough to score an own goal to make the score look respectable. Managers the length and breadth of the country will tell you that results don't matter in pre-season, and that it's about fitness and getting the team to gel. This was as important as ever, as

Wimbledon's new faces had to blend in, and also the new gaffer had to get his own message and style of play across.

In a strange twist of fate the fixture schedule had Wimbledon away on the first day of the season at Watford. Their former manager Dave Bassett had turned a corner and only gave fleeting mention of his time with Wimbledon in his programme notes.. His new chapter was beginning just as Bobby Gould's was. As expected, many of the new faces started and made their league debuts at Vicarage Road. The team was Beasant, Scales, Phelan, Cork, Thorn, Young, Galliers, Sayer, Fashanu, Sanchez and Fairweather. On a baking-hot day the hosts won thanks to a solitary goal towards the end of the first half. Mark Morris, making his debut for the Hornets after his move across London with Bassett, got a touch on a corner and Luther Blissett knocked the ball in from close range. It says something of the Dons' day that Beasant was picked out as their best player. The target of many a transfer rumour during the summer kept the score low, and even an equaliser in the second half that was correctly ruled out could not inspire a tepid performance.

One bonus on the day was the appearance of Steve Galliers, a firm fan favourite, who had twice been voted as the supporters' player of the year. He had been close to leaving the club for Bristol City and had been on loan to them during the 1986/87 season. After losing his place in the first team to Vinnie Jones, he felt he was still able to play at the top level but during his medical the re-emergence of a knee injury meant the move collapsed. It led to summer surgery and an operation that saw some bone taken off and a warning that he would likely not play until September, but in typical Galliers fashion he battled on and got some game time in pre-season. Far from match fit, he got a call from Gould to say he was part of the manager's plans going forward. 'I was only told at 1.45pm so I didn't have time to worry about my knee,' Galliers said of his shock at being called into the team. 'Afterwards I didn't suffer any reaction so I should be all right.'

The opening home game of the season was just three days later, with league champions Everton the first to visit Plough Lane, and no doubt looking to avenge their FA Cup exit earlier in the calendar year. They too were under new management, Howard Kendall having left for Spanish club Athletic Bilbao. His assistant, Colin Harvey, was promptly promoted into the hot seat of one of the best English clubs over the last handful of seasons. One change was made to the team that lost on the opening day, with Galliers rested for Vaughan Ryan. Alan Cork opened the Dons' goal account for the season with a well-taken header, no surprise there, but Gould's men had to hold on as the Toffees battled back and got a deserved leveller just seven minutes from the end.

The season started with a warning from Gould that rebuffed those who still opposed the way Wimbledon played football. He would tell anyone who cared to listen that there was no rule that stated the game had to be played on the ground with sweeping moves, and that if the quickest route to the opposing goal was a long ball through the air then so be it; Wimbledon were not there to please the purists. The Everton game was proof of that as they dug in to gain their first point of the season. Gould said, 'We fight with the right kind of spirit. Everton were under-strength and I am not happy that we only managed to get a point from them.' It had been a stifling evening with low humidity, but the Dons didn't wilt. Gould and Howe had prepared the team well and could now look forward to the visit of Oxford United, looking for the players to respond to the support from the terraces again. Gould added, '[It] can bring out that five per cent needed to make sure that the victories we all seek are there when we need them.'

In front of the lowest First Division crowd for a Saturday fixture since the Second World War, the 1-1 draw against Oxford was far from a decent game, and it took a rush of blood from the U's goalkeeper Peter Hucker to salvage a point. After saving a penalty inside the first five minutes, Hucker went on to have a good game, until the last minute when he ran from his goal to stop Andy Sayer's advance, but having got around the keeper Sayer's cross was met by Cork who atoned for his earlier penalty miss by nodding home. Again, in post-match interviews Gould had to rebuff questions about the long-ball tactics, and reliance on set pieces, which for the record on this day were dire and Gould called them 'a disgrace'.

The next piece of business was off the field and one of the most high-profile signings by the Dons in many years. Despite Fashanu firing early in pre-season he had yet to get off the mark in league football, the evergreen Cork getting the only goals so far but now perhaps a yard slower than in his prime, so extra firepower was needed. The arrival of Terry Gibson from Manchester United had a £200,000 price tag, a record figure for a Wimbledon signing, and came at a price for the manager too. Gould had known Gibson from his time at Coventry, where he had scored at the rate of almost a goal every other game, so was aware of his eye for goal, as was Ron Atkinson at Manchester United, who was trying to bolster his attacking options for a misfiring side and save his own job in the process.

After an unsuccessful time at Old Trafford, and with Gould looking over his own shortlist of options, with Gibson having an eye on a possible return to London after his time at boyhood club Tottenham Hotspur had been cut short, it was time to make the move. The price tag was higher than what the Dons would normally pay out, and to secure the deal Sam Hammam, who held the purse strings, came up with an incentive. Apparently, sheep's testicles are a delicacy in Lebanon, where the owner came from, and so he took Gould to a swish restaurant in Mayfair. There, he proceeded to order a plate of this finest specialist dish, and said that if the manager could devour the lot he would free up the funds and Gibson would be delivered. It seemed like a fair deal, and armed with vinegar, a temporary iron stomach and determination to get his man, Gould managed to finish them up. Good to his word Hammam coughed up the cash, and the paperwork was completed. 'I admire his ability and I'm pleased he has decided to join us,' Gould said when the deal got over the line. 'He is a high-quality player and, although he didn't get a chance to do well at Old Trafford, I know that he is hungry for success now.'

Gibson went straight into the team for the trip to Derby County, who had broken their transfer record when they signed England international defender Mark Wright from Southampton for £760,000, the centre-back making his debut for the newly promoted Rams. It was hard to keep Cork out the team given his early form, and with the physical presence of Fashanu it was Sayer who was left out, while Brian Gayle came into the back four. The Dons were all over Derby from the start and struck the post on two occasions, then Peter Shilton was on good form to keep the game goalless at the break. Derby didn't offer much in attack, and with Wimbledon's pressure building it was Fashanu's first goal of the season that gave them the three points, and sent the majority of the 15,000 crowd home unhappy. Home form was still disappointing though and through the first half against Charlton Athletic, the Dons did little to inspire. The visitors could well have had the points wrapped up by the interval but some poor finishing let them down. Both teams managed a goal and it was even at half-time but the second half was a complete contrast and whatever Gould and Howe had said to their players certainly did the trick. Cork's header and then two goals in as many minutes from Fashanu gave the game a lopsided look, but the five minutes in which the goals came showed how quickly the Dons could turn on the style.

At Newcastle United, the Dons were now in a groove and back to their reputation of fearing no one. Mirandinha may have been the new sensation on Tyneside, but the Brazilian must have wondered what he'd walked into. St James' Park was going through a huge renovation with the main West Stand a building site as the Samba star made his hugely anticipated home debut after his record club transfer. It seemed that all clubs were making big-money moves. There was a quickfire double as Wimbledon were 2-0 up inside ten minutes to put the party on ice. The first had a small piece of fortune as Fashanu's well-struck effort came back off the woodwork and off goalkeeper Martin Thomas. Moments after the restart, Cork hit an even better effort that didn't need any assistance. The Toon Army would have to wait a bit longer for their new man to shine, but it wouldn't be long before he and Paul Gascoigne would start to gel, and even though a late penalty – won by Gazza when he was fouled by Sanchez – did create a tense finish, it was the Dons who secured a third win in a week and they were now up to fifth place, just a point off second.

What was most pleasing was how the defence was playing. Sometimes it could take a few games for new faces to work together and get a good understanding of how they operate as individuals as well as a unit. Eric Young was proving to be a solid and dependable centre-back, and with Scales and Phelan the Dons had full-backs who would be up and down the pitch, supporting the play as well as keeping the opposing threat quiet. Further testament to how well the back line was working came when Andy Thorn received a late call to join the England under-21 squad in Germany. 'It's a great personal honour but it is down to a large extent to the fact that I've been helped by the other Wimbledon players. Because of the way we play, people don't give us enough credit, but I think my selection is a step forward,' Thorn said. Sadly the England team lost 2-0, but Thorn would be ready for the next call-up.

One face now missing from the Richardson Evans training sessions was Steve Galliers. Having fought his way back into recognition, it was with a reluctance that Gould let Galliers go and with Bristol City keeping an eye on his progress he ended up going to the Robins just a month after the initial talks had broken down.

It was early days in the league, but the signs were promising. The fitness was never in question with this group, but now they had good organisation and tactical preparation. Don Howe would work tirelessly with the squad each day, honing their skillsets. It was a good job that the team were at peak fitness as the games kept coming fast, and by the end of September they had been tested with a home match against West Ham United, and trips to Arsenal and Portsmouth, plus a League Cup tie away at Rochdale.

There was a mixed bag of results to reward the miles clocked up. An unchanged side from the one that won at Newcastle then played out a 1-1 draw with the Hammers, and as you would expect of a derby it was a feisty affair, with Mark Ward getting his marching orders after an elbow made contact with Dennis Wise in a not-so-legal fashion, and a handful of yellow cards were shown. This was after Wise had opened the scoring, capping off some good work by Fashanu, and the Dons were left regretting not converting more chances, as well as Cork hitting the post. Just past the hour Tony Cottee scored a deserved goal. 'It's always nice to set up goals,' Wise said, 'but I do want to score more and that means poaching a bit more. I am at a bit of a disadvantage because I ring the box for corners and free kicks which restricts my chances a bit.'

At Arsenal the team never got going after falling behind early to a penalty decision when Wise was adjudged to have clipped Perry Groves. The spot kick from Michael Thomas was neatly tucked away, and then Alan Smith's finish and an own goal by Andy Thorn, who deflected a David Rocastle effort in, meant the game was effectively over at half-time.

Through the rise up the divisions the Dons had met with Portsmouth a few times in both league and cup competitions, and the last time had been in the fourth round of the FA Cup in 1986/87, a routine win for the Londoners. Perhaps then some complacency had crept into their play down on the south coast. Pompey were not going to submit to the physical style that the Dons had used to win that match, and this led to some rough challenges from both teams. Alan Ball knew that the only way his side could come away with any points was to match the physicality, and he would have been pleased with his team's efforts over the 90 minutes which resulted in a late winner. 'It was blood and thunder all right, but we matched them in every department,' Ball mused afterwards. Gould was less than impressed, though, saying, 'The old Wimbledon would never have conceded [Lee] Sandford's goal.' Referring to the Portsmouth full-back's strike five minutes from time, he added, 'But the new Wimbledon have been together for only nine games.'

It had looked like Wimbledon were back to winning ways at Fratton Park after a Sanchez header from close range put them ahead, but it only took ten minutes for Micky Quinn to level things up with a tidy finish beyond Beasant. Sandford held his run long enough as Wimbledon tried to apply a poorly executed offside trap at a free kick, and he was able to coolly finish for his first goal to set the chimes off and secure the points for Pompey. The game saw Vinnie Jones's first start of the season. The midfielder had some minor surgery on his knee during the summer and took over duties in the middle from Vaughan Ryan who had ably deputised but was always going to play second fiddle to the enforcer.

This drop in form was reflected in the table as the Dons slipped to tenth at the end of September and saw their League Cup tie finely balanced after a 1-1 draw at Rochdale. The Fourth Division side had nothing to lose and saw this as an opportunity for an upset, in which the Dons were gifted a penalty to give the game balance. In the return leg Wimbledon had to survive the dismissal of Eric Young, after the big defender lost control of an elbow at the start of the second half. Rochdale immediately took advantage with a headed goal and the upset was on. Having had two goals chalked off the Dons at last made a breakthrough when another goalkeeping error led to a Fashanu goal, and when Cork made it two a handful of minutes later it completed the comeback. Gould was happy with the attitude of those who finished the game, but knew that more of the same would be needed in the coming month.

Gould knew that even with his new players settling in well, he had to be on his guard and not let standards slip. The Arsenal result had been unacceptable, and it needed harsh words but calm heads to try and steady the ship. The subsequent results did little to impress and with a potentially tough autumn ahead, it was time to roll the sleeves up and get back to basics. 'At the end of the day the game is about 11 men against 11 men and making sure that we make less mistakes than the opposition,' he stated in his programme notes before the game against the surprising league leaders, Queens Park Rangers.

Always ones to bounce back and put the noses out of joint of more revered opposition, Wimbledon had the chance to do just that. Jim Smith had his team well drilled but knew this would be the hardest test of the season so far, and in a bruising encounter it was the visitors who took the win, even if they left with several players feeling the pain for their efforts. The game was decided after the hour with two quick goals, a good strike from Gary Bannister putting the R's ahead then after Terry Fenwick scored from the spot it looked like the points were won. A late Fashanu goal wasn't enough to rescue a draw, this despite the Dons being in the ascendency and showing more ambition. It was a little ironic that QPR won the game with two 'Wimbledon-style' goals, earning a smash-and-grab win. 'We knew what to expect, and it was up to the players to take care of themselves. They did that very well indeed,' Smith said afterwards.

The match also saw the full return of Vinnie Jones, but unfortunately it was his tackle on Kevin Brock that led to the winning penalty: 'I had run all the way back from the 18-yard box to our six-yard area and I was a bit tired. He [Brock] did well but if I hadn't been so tired I don't think I'd have conceded the penalty,' said Jones. Fitness was always going to be an issue after a long period of time out. His operation in May to remove a cyst was successful but also had complications after in regard to swelling that delayed his recovery, but heads were still high and looking ahead to an important run of games. Jones said, 'We came in the following day to discuss the game but weren't too despondent. Bobby pointed out a few things that were going wrong, but he also told us that we were only one point short of the total Wimbledon had after ten games last year.'

The eagerly awaited match against title favourites Liverpool was postponed due to a flooded pitch, and that might have been a blessing in disguise given the dip in form, so next up was a trip to Kenilworth Road, the home of Luton Town's plastic pitch. This could have been the perfect platform to get the Dons back on track, but instead they failed to score despite hitting the woodwork on three occasions. 'We got the lucky breaks,' Luton manager Ray Harford said. Some stuttering play in the back line left Brian Stein free, after good attacking work, to open the scoring after half an hour. Danny Wilson ensured the points stayed with the home team in the early stages of the second period. This gave Wimbledon their fourth defeat in a row, and from their promising start they were now in 13th. 'You make your own luck. We've got to work hard all the time, but John Fashanu was truly magnificent,' said Gould. It's not often that a player gets singled out after a loss, but the manager wanted the rest of his squad to apply themselves the same way his striker had been. 'I've been

Fashanu's manager for 12 games and couldn't have asked for a better player. If a few more people were like him, we wouldn't be blaming our luck for our poor results,' he added. Nevertheless, the current run was alarming, and there was no let-up in the fixtures.

Newcastle United were the Dons' next League Cup opponents after Gould's team had made heavy work of getting past Rochdale over two legs, with the tie at Plough Lane. Terry Phelan was out with a hamstring pull which meant a call-up for 18-year-old Kevin Bedford, and even though he had a solid debut it was the emergence of Terry Gibson that grabbed the headlines. Brian Gayle was still in the back four, keeping his place after Eric Young's sending off in the previous round, and Vaughan Ryan was back in ahead of Jones. Gibson had started the season well but was yet to get on the scoresheet, but in front of a busy crowd on a misty evening he finally notched his first goal as a Don.

Fashanu scored first, his goal coming after a drop by Kelly in the Toon goal, but the visitors were back in the tie just before the half-time whistle blew. Dave Beasant brought down Darren Jackson for an easy decision, and Neil McDonald scored the penalty. Newcastle were the better of the two teams and it took some fine saves from Beasant to keep the score level, not least when Paul Gascoigne looked certain to score. 'I've always spoken very highly of "Lurch", and in my book he is one of the country's top goalkeepers,' said a relieved Gould after the game finished. The tie was odds-on for a replay as it went deep into stoppage time but that was when Gibson pounced. Ryan headed the ball on, and substitute John Gannon fired over a cross which was met at the near post with a neatly flicked header past Kelly. 'I really did need that goal. After 18 months of getting my confidence battered at United and going so many games without a goal here I did begin to wonder,' the tiny striker gleefully said.

With the bottle uncorked the goals started to flow and Gibbo soon got the second in a 3-0 rout of Tottenham Hotspur at White Hart Lane. He said, 'When I came here [Wimbledon] I had to adapt to a style which is entirely different to what I had played at United where it was a short passing game. That wasn't really my game and I had to change. It didn't work out but now I'm back to the way I used to play and enjoy playing best.' Fashanu looped a header to make it 1-0, then came the Gibson goal that was greeted with such emotion from all the team that the referee had to break up the pile-on. Gannon later scored the third goal. 'We well deserved our win. We worked hard for it, and much of the credit goes to our coach Don Howe,' Gould told the reporting press afterwards. 'We still want to blitz people, but thanks to Don, we are learning to be patient.'

The first meeting of the season against Liverpool was one which would end in stalemate. Ray Houghton had entered the action on the hour and soon opened the scoring when he received a short pass and then waltzed through the Dons' defence, courtesy of a lucky bounce off Gayle, to slot calmly past Beasant. But in a sign off things to come Wimbledon would not just roll over and with 15 minutes left they got a point. Some good link-up play from Fairweather, Fashanu and Gibson on the right led to a cross by Fash, which ended up with a fierce Ryan strike towards goal, but it was heading well wide before Fairweather deflected the ball and directed it out of the reach of a diving Bruce Grobbelaar.

After the Liverpool game, which had the largest crowd of the season so far even though it was in midweek, the Dons got back to winning ways with a comfortable home victory against Southampton on a day that told you winter was well and truly on its way. Fairweather scored again, another scrappy effort but they all count, and even though the Saints had a decent amount of possession they rarely threatened to equalise. When Alan Cork latched on to a sloppy back-pass he was clean through and beat John Burridge in the closing minutes. The two goalscorers had swapped places on the pitch and bench but showed that they were both still up to the task when called on.

The trip to Coventry then saw Ian Hazel make his debut as Vaughan Ryan was sidelined with a broken jaw. This was the first game of the season that the 19-year-old had not been involved in, proving a very capable stand-in for Vinnie Jones, and it was a setback as he had formed a solid combination with Sanchez in the middle of the pitch. The cold Midlands air must have affected referee George Tyson's vision at first when he was adamant that Thorn had handled when for all others it was clear the ball struck him in the chest. The spot kick was thumped home by Brian Kilcline, not put off by the hard protests that saw both Beasant and Gayle booked. The second half started with a Fashanu masterclass as he first scored, then set up Wise to get the Dons ahead, and finally he stretched his big frame to score again with a wonderful diving header. This all happened within ten minutes, just after the hour, and the game was won. But when David Speedie scored with five minutes left some panic set in. City had lost six straight games and were fighting for everything, then with the whistle being raised to Tyson's lips Coventry attacked one last time. Dave Phillips escaped Fashanu and crossed for Micky Gynn to score. 'Excellent finishing, but he didn't close Phillips down before the last goal. I'll be showing him the video!' Bobby Gould said of Fashanu.

The treatment table was in full use now with two high-profile players looking set to be out for a few weeks. Terry Gibson had not played since the draw against Liverpool after suffering a pelvic injury, and Vaughan Ryan was still feeling the effects of the hairline fracture to his jaw. To add insult to injuries the Dons crashed out of the League Cup at Oxford United, their luck finally running out. They fell behind as early as the fifth minute when a lightning turn by Dean Saunders enabled him to get by Gayle and his shot gave Beasant no chance. After the shock opening Wimbledon grew into the game but were lacking that instinctive edge in front of goal. Oxford were relying on counter-attacks and with Saunders they always carried a goal threat, but it was the evergreen Cork who tied the game up halfway through the second half with a typical headed goal. However, this failed to inspire his team-mates and instead of trying to win the game they let Oxford back into it, and when Gayle was sloppy in possession, Les Phillips scored the winner to put the Dons out of the first domestic cup competition of the season.

As December approached, Wimbledon were comfortably in the top half of the table and could for the moment settle into the league fixtures before the FA Cup started. No better way to get over a domestic cup exit than a visit of one of the most famous teams in the world, Manchester United, who were sitting just above the Dons in the league. United had, however, been beaten twice by Wimbledon in the previous season, and as they were always guaranteed to swell the average attendance with their away support and casual neutrals, Plough Lane was full to see a mainly uneventful game for an hour or so. Then it was Clayton Blackmore who drew first blood, although maybe that also went to the Viv Anderson–John Fashanu battle that went on all afternoon. The young midfielder scored with United's first attempt on target, and with their 11-game unbeaten run looking like it was to be extended, the goal only acted as a match to the blue touchpaper. 'Wimbledon's power and physique is difficult to handle. Everyone knows what to expect when you come here,' Alex Ferguson said after the game when his team buckled under late pressure. Fashanu had been a nuisance all afternoon and as the floodlights shone brightly, he also burst into life with a wicked shot that came back off the post and into the path of in-form Fairweather, who tucked the ball home.

The winning goal was fitting for a scrappy game that would offer little to the purist, but that was typical Wimbledon. What wasn't typical was the source. Just two minutes of the 90 remained when left-back John Scales was in an advanced position with a sight of goal. He let fly with an ambitious shot that took a flick off two defending players to leave goalkeeper Gary Walsh helpless. 'It was a fantastic feeling. I thought I had taken too long over the shot because the United players were closing me down, so I was relieved when the ball went in,' said Scales after the game when reacting to his first goal for the Dons. This was what Wimbledon were all about, up and in people's faces. They had never cared for reputations before, and they still didn't.

This was backed up when they went to Stamford Bridge a week later to take on a Chelsea side that were unbeaten at home so far. After a first half that barely drew a ripple from those in attendance, it was Wimbledon who reacted better to any half-time heat. Fairweather could and perhaps should have scored with an attempt that was cleared off the line, and when a Sanchez header came back off the post, Wise was in the right place to net.

Wimbledon's ill discipline, however, was starting to grate on Bobby Gould, and he would address it in his next programme notes, as the yellow card count for the season was closing in on 40. It was this brandishing of cards that cost the Dons another famous win at Stamford Bridge. Brian Gayle received his call for an early bath when remonstrating with the official on the side of the pitch too hard and long, and this was after his captain Beasant had seen yellow for bringing down Tony Dorigo, although it was said afterwards that the abuse aimed at the linesman wasn't for the foul, but the possible offside position Gordon Durie was in during the build-up. Durie, after the lengthy delay to sort out the shuffling cards, kept his nerve to gain a share of the points. Fairweather also saw red for a nasty challenge.

'The referee and linesman are just as human as they are,' Gould said in his programme notes of his players' reaction to the Chelsea incident, and others that had caused over-the-top responses, 'and those individuals, like the players, will make mistakes. It is always easy to question other people's mistakes, but there are also correct manners in which we would like to ask certain questions and as we are involved in very emotional happenings on a football pitch, we must be aware of the responsibility for the quickness of tongues and speech.'

Eric Young had returned to the side against Chelsea at the expense of Clive Goodyear; the pair had both been out for several games for different reasons, Young being suspended and then finding it hard to come back into the team, whereas Goodyear had been injured. Gayle was suspended after his red card at Stamford Bridge but both defenders were back in the side by the time Wimbledon travelled to Hillsborough to play Sheffield Wednesday. Before that, the Dons had gained a draw at home to Brian Clough's Nottingham Forest. Clough's teams played clever, neat, precise football, and this current crop were young and being drilled into what he hoped were the next set of silverware winners. After the warnings to be better behaved in high-profile situations, the Wimbledon players were choirboys when five minutes before half-time Neil Webb tussled with Dennis Wise and the latter went to ground in the area. It looked like a nailed-on penalty, but instead of waving their arms in furious appeal the Dons abided by the non-decision by Howard Taylor, which almost caught them cold as Nigel, son of Brian, raced forward and set up Calvin Plummer, who shot high and wide. 'I thought it was a penalty and was very surprised when the ref didn't give it, but we have been told to watch it, so we did,' Wise recalled.

Clough junior had already scored midway through the first half following a neat take-down and finish as his dad looked for a first win over Wimbledon. Just before the hour, however, a short throw caught out the Forest defence and Wise swirled over a cross that became a shot which deceived Steve Sutton in goal and dipped under the bar. With the game coming to an end the most surprising event was that not one card had been shown to a Wimbledon player, and that was a perfect result for Gould after waxing lyrical about the importance of discipline.

The following week, that shuffled back line was joined by a makeshift midfield as Gannon and Hazel came in for Fairweather and Cork. Wednesday were in a relegation scrap and needed the points, and this was reflected in the balance of play. Lee Chapman flicked a header past Beasant for the game's only goal with just under 20 minutes left. 'We were very, very poor. That performance didn't epitomise the spirit at Wimbledon as I know it. The attitude was all wrong,' a despondent Gould reported after the match.

The Wembley trail was about to begin on two fronts. As part of the Football Association centenary celebrations, the Mercantile Credit Centenary Festival was to be held beneath the Twin Towers on a weekend in the middle of April. Teams from all four divisions had a chance to play as to qualify they had to be at the top of their form table from 1 November through 15 games, or by the end of February. In total 16 teams would play in full 11-a-side matches, with shortened halves of 20 minutes each way in the first two rounds, and 30-minute halves in the semi-finals and final. In an innovation to encourage attacking play, no extra time would be played and instead corner kicks would decide the winner of a drawn match. The top eight teams in the First Division would qualify for the festival, and at this time Wimbledon were sitting comfortably in one of those top spots.

The other route to Wembley was the more historical one, and one that Wimbledon were primed for. Their first opponents in the 1987/88 FA Cup would be West Bromwich Albion at home, and on paper this looked an easy win. The Baggies were managed by Ron Atkinson but were struggling near the foot of the Second Division, and they had also not won a domestic cup game away from The Hawthorns for four years. A cup run for them would be a bonus distraction from their league form but could also be a hindrance in their bid for survival, something that Wimbledon didn't have to worry about, and they still had a handful of games to navigate before the FA Cup dreams could start.

The Christmas week started with Norwich City down at Plough Lane. Fashanu bagged his 11th goal of the season, a header finishing off a move started by Wise's cross and a flick-on by Fairweather. This came on the 15-minute mark, and despite new Canary Robert Fleck's debut after his £500,000 move from Rangers, the visitors had Bryan Gunn to thank as he kept his team in the game with a few good saves, in front of the lowest attendance in First Division history, 4,096. Gould had been back to the piggy bank and raided it to the tune of £15,000 to acquire the services of Robbie Turner from Bristol Rovers. The 21-year-old striker was seen as handy cover for the Dons' attackers, and given that John Fashanu had admiring eyes turning his way, with several scouts keeping a close watch on his growing reputation for goals, Turner could also have been seen as a natural successor. 'He has got terrific aerial qualities. I had analysed the forward situation after coming to the club and realised that there was no one to replace John if he was injured. Robbie fits that bill,' said Gould.

Both West Ham and Spurs had their top men in the stands at Plough Lane for the last game and would have seen the prolific target man get substituted for Turner, making the new man the 100th player to pull on a Dons shirt in the Football League. Fashanu's back had been giving him problems, but this aside it was perhaps the Hammers boss John Lyall who would have been most interested, as Fash could have also been a target to replace Frank McAvennie.

The Dons turned 1987 into 1988 with three great wins, two at home and one away, and goals aplenty as they warmed up for the FA Cup third round. First off Arsenal, who were harbouring hopes of a title run, were comprehensively beaten 3-1, a result that meant the Dons were only six points behind their more illustrious north London neighbours. The discipline that had been called into question by so many of the nation's media, and some at the FA, was again a focus as no players in blue shirts were booked, making it four out of the last five games that the referee didn't have to reach for his notebook. This was a first win over the Gunners, and you'd have been forgiven for thinking it was the Dons who were potential title contenders, although they did have to overcome a David Rocastle goal midway through the first half. Arsenal would only have one more attempt on target, and instead they had to endure lots of Wimbledon pressure which resulted in a second-half demolition. Dennis Wise crossed for Alan Cork to plant his header past John Lukic in the first minute after the restart, and then roles were reversed just a couple of minutes later as Cork gathered a loose ball and Wise scored from inside the area. The Dons played flowing football, and this wasn't a surprise to those in and around the squad as they knew the talent they had, but they were often victims of their physical style, and having that stigma was hard to shake off. Why should they, though; this was their strength after all, the cavalier one-for-all-and-all-for-one approach. Now, by keeping clear heads they were getting the plaudits. Jones got the third in the last minute, a simple finish after good work by Sanchez.

On New Year's Day they beat Derby County 2-1. Once again they fell behind, but their spirit and dogged enthusiasm kept them going. Cork headed the equaliser, and just after the hour Fashanu hit a fierce winner.

The next day they travelled to the Manor Ground, and the almost perfect festive period of games was complete with a thrashing of Oxford United. Not even the wind and rain could stop Wimbledon on the day, as Oxford, who had not won a game since dumping the Dons out of the League Cup, were blown away. Fairweather punished a dithering Peter Hucker for the first, then Sanchez scored following a trademark run and header to double the lead, with Fashanu making it 3-0 at the break. Dean Saunders was still Oxford's main goal threat and he tucked away a penalty but had a second saved, Young conceding both. Before Beasant's fine spot-kick save, the Dons scored a fourth, Cork on hand to poke the ball in after some simply terrible defending. It was easy to see why Oxford were struggling at the wrong end of the table, and even though they did get one more back the predatory instincts of Cork made it a nap hand. The result was Wimbledon's first five-goal game in the top division and it took them up to fifth in the table. Some in the media were talking about the Dons being in Europe the following season, should the ban on English clubs be lifted. They were only three points off second-placed Nottingham Forest, albeit Clough's men had three games in hand, but the form and spirit were now back in place following a tepid autumn. All eyes and focus now turned to the FA Cup.

Could they match, or even better, their run from the year before?

The Midfielder's Story
Lawrie Sanchez

'READING GOT promoted the season before from the Fourth Division,' Lawrie Sanchez recalled when asked about how he came to sign for Wimbledon. 'I was second-leading scorer from midfield, had a really good season. I went to see the manager to see if I could get a rise of £15, and you'd be lucky if you got £10, and you'd be happy. That's what it was like in those days. The manager asked "how'd you think you did", I said I had a good season, and he said, "I don't think you played that well," and at that moment my mouth dropped. I just thought "I've got no future here." I'd been there eight years. The manager, Ian Branfoot, had taken over halfway through the season when we were third or fourth in the league. I left there with a £5 rise and thought stuff it, but in those days, you didn't have freedom of contract. Basically they owned your contract; you look back and you wonder how that ever occurred.' Dispirited by Branfoot's comments, Sanchez tried to remain upbeat. 'I'd have been in a fantastic position if it were this day and age, I was 26, fit and healthy and playing every game. I had over 300 appearances by that time. I was a goalscoring midfielder, box-to-box, 6ft 2in, can do all sorts. The new season started, and I was in and out of the team, he was mucking me about. He wanted me out for whatever reason.'

Then Sanchez was hit with a bombshell. 'I came into training, and he said, "You're going to Swindon." I asked what do you mean, and he said, "I've agreed a deal with Swindon for you." I'd been at the club since I was a schoolboy, so I didn't want to go anywhere. It was my hometown team, I was happy. I lived in the town ten minutes from training. I was a local boy; this was my team. Anyway, I went down to Lou Macari at Swindon, bemused, "What do I do? I don't really want to come here." I had a chat with my partner at the time and she said, "Well, they want you out."

'Swindon offered me a rise, they were in the Fourth Division, Reading just got promotion to the Third, and Wimbledon were in the Second. So I'm sat at home that night feeling sorry for myself and got a call from a guy called Vince Craven and he said he'd heard that Reading are trying to get rid of me and "not to sign for Swindon, whatever you do". He told me to come and have a chat with Dave Bassett, and that he wants to talk to you tonight at the Hilton Heathrow, by the side of the airport. So I get up there and was sat in reception. His assistant came across to me, Alan Gillett; he said, "Hello, Harry will be here in a minute." I'm sat there thinking, "Who the fuck is Harry, I want to speak to Dave Bassett!" Soon after, Harry turns up. He sits me down at a table and asked what have Swindon offered me, a bit naive I told him what it was. "Oh yeah! We'll match that, don't worry." He's shouting out figures and other people around us were listening to the conversation, and I'm like "be a bit quiet" but anyway I agreed.

'Second Division, I thought a year or two there, see how it goes, play at that level. I can test myself at that level, so I signed for the same money I would have signed for Swindon in the Fourth. I asked him what to do next, and he said "get your boots and come in tomorrow, don't worry about going back". So I went to the Reading training ground the following day to pick my boots up and Branfoot called me and asked what I was doing. "I'm going." "Swindon?" he asked. I said, "Nah, I'm not going to Swindon; you'll get a phone call later in the morning, you deal with it.'"

Sanchez was ready to see beyond Reading. 'So I got my stuff, went to Wimbledon and started training and the deal was sorted out between the Dons and Reading. It was their first season in the Second Division. I watched a game in early December, and I thought "bloody hell, they're good". From where I came from to this level of football, how do I get into this team? When I made my debut, I came in at half-time, Bassett's gone to me, "You fucking fit or what?!" I looked at him as if to say it's my debut, I'm doing my best. "You fucking need to liven up," and that was my introduction to Wimbledon. A new way of life. Reading is the sticks compared to Wimbledon. It was dog-eat-dog and you had to be smart, had to be clever, you had to be verbally adept in training, you had to understand what was going on. There was so much more to the game at Wimbledon than there had been at Reading which I'd been cocooned in for so many years, so initially it was quite daunting, but once I got into it I thought this suits me and I can play in this, and I became an integral part of the team for ten years.'

Settling in at the Dons wasn't always easy, but Sanchez was confident in his ability, and once in the team he became a regular. 'The first full season

I was like a house on fire. I scored nine goals if you include the one that was disallowed against Bradford in an abandoned game, top scorer behind Alan Cork. Wimbledon suited me, I was confident, the camaraderie suited me. I wasn't at the forefront of what went on, but I enjoyed the banter and everything that went with it. I enjoyed the sense of this is what a team is supposed to be, and we were the epitome of what a team is supposed to be, on the field and off the field, to a certain extent. Although in the latter years it became a bit more pastiche. The team hung together, played together when we crossed the white line, we were a team. We knew each other's jobs, we did each other's jobs, and we looked after each other on the field. There was 11 leaders out there.

'When Bobby Gould took over, he got me, Dave [Beasant], and Corky together and said, "I know what you lot do, but I don't know the ins and outs, but I want you lot to keep doing what you do." Then Don Howe said, "I don't like what you do, I don't like your direct play, I don't like your intent, but I'll look at what you do and try and make you better at it, in the way you do things as players and formations, not in the physicality." He adapted to what we did. This was the England coach, and I think he learned as much from Wimbledon as he taught us to an extent.

We were strong characters and we led that team to the cup final with a new manager, and Gouldy was very good at bringing in players like Eric Young, Terry Phelan and John Scales. Sam Hammam said to me about Wimbledon, "Dario Gradi sorted out the youth system there that brought so many good players like Kevin Gage, Paul Fishenden, all those young players that came into the first team. Bassett came in after him and gave it the against the wall type attitude that Dons had, then Bobby came in and bought very well for the club.'"

In 1987 the Dons were knocked out at the quarter-final stage of the FA Cup, but this was a good learning curve and Sanchez could see that the team were ready. 'We were disappointed we lost to Spurs, we believed we could beat them. We beat them away from home in our first season with Hoddle and Waddle, and the entertainers. At our place this would do us, but they scored from a free kick late on. We got to the quarter-finals and were disappointed, but it did give us a feel that the cup is something we can possibly win. Don said to us, "You only get ten runs at this during your career assuming you're fit and everything so take every run seriously as you never know," and I remember him saying that at the beginning of the run. You always think there's next year but there isn't as you might be injured the following season. We were full of beans after finishing sixth and we didn't fear anybody by that stage. We'd won away at Liverpool, Manchester United, Spurs, and when they'd come to our place we'd smash them as well. We were bang on ready for it.'

The FA Cup run started with 'an easy game' against West Bromwich Albion, but then, as Sanchez takes up the story, 'We were up against it at Mansfield. It was a boggy pitch; we were struggling then Phelan got the winner in a game we were lucky to come out of. A horrible game.' Next came the drama at Newcastle, 'I had a massive row with Don in the changing room afterwards; he didn't like the stuff we'd do on and off the ball. They'd do runs and we'd just block them, especially in midfield. If they tried to make blindside runs, we'd just stop them, but not in a legal way, and we did bits and pieces. We'd time-waste when we scored goals. People would go down injured, and it took five minutes to restart the game. We had a statistic that teams concede within the next five minutes, so we had a thing that once we scored we'd put the ball to bed. Someone would get it and whack it into the crowd, or someone would lie down, and the physio would come on. It used to be five minutes before the game started again, especially away from home. At home we'd probably start the game quicker as we had momentum and get another quite quickly, but we were just trying to stop the run of the game. Don hated all that, he was clean-cut. It was nasty stuff but when you look back it happened all the time, but we took it to the next level, it was part of our levelling the field up. We didn't have the wage packets or ability to match others, but we could match them in the physicality and dark arts. He took it personally and I had a stand-up row with him. He said, "You got to cut all this stuff out." I told him back, "Don, we just beat Newcastle, 3-1 away, what other teams have you been at that do that!" Then Mirandinha came in, he sent some flowers in for Dave as he kicked him up the backside and had chased him around the pitch. It was a great win, even then they were a big club.'

Next up were Watford in the quarter-final, and the half-time team talk took a new twist and cut the tension as Wimbledon were 1-0 down and reduced to ten men. Sanchez said, 'I sat next to Corky in the dressing room. Eric was coming on. It was the end of Gayley, and the beginning of Eric's career if you want as they switched the number one in the role at centre-back. Gayle left at the end of the season, and wrongly in my opinion he was left out the cup final squad as he was going by then as freedom of contract had come in. Anyway, everyone realised it was Corky coming off when the sub had to be made, it was obvious it was him that had to make way for Eric to come on so we were doing the team talk and Corky's gone, "Gouldy, fucking hell, are you going to tell me I'm actually off!" It hadn't actually been said; everyone just assumed. We all just creased up.'

After Young got the winner, it was off to White Hart Lane for the semi-final. 'Gouldy drove the minibus and was stopped and asked "where's the rest of the team?" when he got there. He told them they're coming in their cars, and we all came from different parts of London and arrived at the ground. Nottingham Forest and Liverpool [in the other semi-final], you couldn't get a ticket, but ours you could pay on the gate! It was a strange game as Luton weren't a lot bigger than us to be honest, their fanbase was a bit bigger but not an awful lot. They lost to Reading in the Simod Cup Final and I remember thinking I could be at Wembley myself in a month if we beat Luton and we did. We expected to beat them. It wasn't a great game, but we were good enough on the day and were pleased that was the draw we got.'

With several games to go in a tightly packed end to the season, some players were notable absentees, but not Sanchez at first. 'I was a bit naive to be fair. I played every game that season, I was turning up and playing and not realising that one or two other players were thinking, "That'll do me, I've got the cup final, we're safe in the league, so I'll look after myself," and against Chelsea at home I scored and I'm looking around thinking "where's the rest of the team?" A few sat it out. It would be interesting to look at those team sheets after the semi-final to see how many missed games, but I wanted to play every game in those days and score goals. I just enjoyed playing rather than training or being on the treatment table.'

One of the fables surrounding the build-up to the big game was the evening before, and when asked for his version of events Sanchez was quick to correct, 'The proper version of that night you mean. Some of the players had just been to have their hair cut. I had mine cut in the week for some reason and this time it was very short, and one or two others decided to have theirs done that night, no idea where they disappeared to. Me and Dave [Beasant] said to the gaffer, "We've finished training, we've had dinner, it's a long night, we can't just sit about here. Do you mind if we wander down to the pub just to break it up?" I think he gave Dave £50 or something and said have a drink on me so me and Dave and five or six of us wander down. Clive, Scalesy, we got to the pub which was the original changing rooms of the team when they played on Wimbledon Common. We had a shandy, nothing more as we had a game the next day! They brought down a woman from next door whose father had played for the club. She was in her 70s so we were talking; he would have played on the Common! She sat there and we had a laugh with the locals. We were there an hour tops and we wandered back. It just killed some time. No one was pissed. I read stories about how they drunk themselves silly, but I didn't see it. The little group I was in certainly wasn't.'

Was this a myth busted? The hype had well and truly got to the team and the few days leading up to that night, and indeed the journey to the stadium were recalled as something of a novelty experience, such as the television cameras aboard the coach to Wembley. 'It played up to those who liked it, Vinnie, Wisey, the bigger [characters], [to] the rest of us it was just a laugh and a joke. It was an interference, but it took away some of the pressure, it gave you something else to think about other than the game. We would be driving up to Wembley and it was all red, there was no blue around. We had a fanbase of 5,500 and we were given 22,500 tickets and half those ended up with Liverpool fans. It was

100 degrees pitchside, the hottest day of the year. It finally hit me at 3pm when the ref blew the whistle and I was thinking, "Bloody hell, we got another 90 minutes of the season left here." You're taken in by all the other stuff that's going on. We were on the BBC *Clothes Show* with Jeff Banks showing off our Top Man suits, model those at Plough Lane too, and the wives modelling their stuff. A whole rigmarole of build-up.'

To the match itself, and the confidence was clear in the team, 'We fancied ourselves in the game, we were the last team to win at Anfield, and if we did what we could do, they didn't cause us that many problems. Wisey doubled up with Clive, so he wasn't left one-on-one with [John] Barnes, and we kept the ball away from [Alan] Hansen as he was the ball player out of defence, so isolate him and let [Gary] Gillespie have it more. They were the two things that we focused on, and be good at set plays which we were. [Peter] Beardsley got a goal but it was disallowed. I said to Dave after, "You didn't need to dive for that, you just made it look more realistic."'

And for Wimbledon's goal itself, the scorer was filling a gap; it could have been very different, 'I used to be three or four in the wall. Corky would be one and he was, then Fash, and with Young around the back, and Thorn behind Fash, then me. Fash was slow coming up, so I stepped up into second and I got the touch. We weren't lined up as we should have been but at the end of the day I was in the right position.'

The contentious penalty decision was the next incident to get over, 'Dave, Clive, and those near the ball were angry that it had been given. Once he saved it everyone thought it was over, so after that we went through the motions. When the penalty was saved, I think Liverpool realised it was not going to be their day and this team had got them today, and I think we fully deserved it to be fair. They ran out of ideas.'

The final whistle was the end of the journey, but the dreams of every child still had to be made real, of getting the cup and parading it. 'We worked our butts off that day. I don't think we realised the significance of it; at the time it was a win. We'd won the final but didn't realise what winning the final was at that time, it was just we done what we came to do. The satisfaction of – OK, a job well done. I'm not emotional at the best of times so I thought, "That's not bad, scoring the winner in the final; parents here to see it, so that's quite good." By the time we'd done our celebrations and got our medals, the stadium was empty. [A crowd of] 98,000 and 80,000 of those were Liverpool, so they weren't going to wait to see us get our medals so by the time we were doing our lap of honour we were doing it to an empty stadium. Takes away a little bit as we're like, who are we waving to, so that was quite novel.'

It wasn't just the fans who emptied out quickly – the opposition changing room was also quiet. 'By the time me and Dave went in to swap our shirts, Liverpool had left the stadium, so how quick they were out I don't know, but it was quick! As we didn't get to swap shirts, the following season at the Charity Shield where I was captain, I said to Kenny [Dalglish], "Is there any chance of swapping shirts?" He said, "I'd love to mate, but these are the only ones we've got." Kit suppliers were useless then, and it used to be a real scramble to get your kit. He said, "We need this for the first day of the season so we'll do it when you come to Anfield," but by that time the team had changed so much, so it was just forgotten. We never got to swap shirts apart from Dave and Grobbelaar.'

The dust had settled and it was time to head back to Plough Lane for a post-game party. Win or lose, this was a great achievement to celebrate. 'Everything at the club was ad hoc and cheaply done, a penny here and there, but that day we had a marquee on the pitch. So you came down the tunnel into it, each player had a table for their family of eight or ten. The *Match of the Day* studio was set up in the corner with Jimmy Hill and Des Lynam, so they were doing the show there. I didn't get a chance to eat as I was chatting and doing interviews. By about 11pm I said to my partner, "I'm ready to go, I'm knackered." We started to leave as my brother was coming down the tunnel. He'd been at the game and had drunk in every pub between there and Wimbledon. He asked what we were doing, I told him I was going to bed as I was falling asleep. I hadn't eaten all day, we didn't eat there, we'd just been drinking champagne, and it was a really hot day. He said, "You can't do that, you scored the winning goal in the final, you've got to celebrate until the dawn chorus." I said, "You stay and celebrate, I can't keep my eyes open, I just need to go to bed," so he stayed. Apparently, he was the last person out the marquee he enjoyed it so much. He had a bet on me at 33/1, and had a tenner on so got £330 which in those days was more bonus than I got, as we didn't have a win bonus in the final.'

Back at the hotel Sanchez enjoyed some much-needed rest, but he also revealed, 'We went back to Cannizaro's which as you know is a posh hotel, and not what we were used to. The doorman said, "Mr Sanchez, would you like a paper in the morning, which one?" I told him every one that's available in the western world! The next morning he knocks on the door and had a foot deep of papers literally, in two hands! We just sat in bed and read all the papers which was fantastic. Then we went for the parade. I said to my brother you can get on the bus for the tour, but I never saw him for a week, he was still celebrating. We started at the hotel and were looking for people to wave at, there's people walking their dogs quietly. But finally we got to the Town Hall square, before that we thought this is going to be embarrassing but at the square, that was great.'

Lawrie Sanchez's winning goal is part of not just Wimbledon FC history, but the history of the wider football world. It will be forever shown in montages of upsets and previews of finals. If he hadn't had that chance phone call and a rushed meeting in a Heathrow hotel then the story may have been different, but as he looks back with fondness on his days with the club this will always be the goal for which he is known. Not bad for someone who was in the wrong position.

Five

Brummies and Boggy Pitches

The Dons Song

We're the boys in blue and yellow
From Wimbledon FC
They say we came from nowhere
Until we went to the top of the league
We're SW19's army
And winning is our game
We'll entertain you evermore
Like we've done at the old Plough Lane

CHORUS:
WE'RE THE DONS
WE'RE THE DONS
WE'RE THE DONS FROM WIMBLEDON FC!

We're the boys in blue and yellow
From Wimbledon FC
Yet now we're on TV

The media sometimes knocks us
But soccer is our game
We aim to score the winning goals
Wherever you see us play

REPEAT CHORUS…

We're the boys in blue and yellow
From Wimbledon FC
We're the giant-killers from the past
And we've been to the top of the league
We're S19's army
And the side we have is strong
So, cheers us through the season's games
Let's hear you sing along!

REPEAT CHORUS…

Alan Cork had scored for the 11th time in 1987/88, and his 150th goal for Wimbledon, during the 5-2 win at Oxford. 'It was a nice way to start the year. Now I'm looking to get my 160th goal to equal the number Bobby Gould scored in his career. Hopefully, I'll be able to do that this season, although, at the moment, I'll be pleased to get to 15,' he said as the Dons prepared for the visit of Ron Atkinson's West Bromwich Albion, a team who had snapped a ten-game run without a win when they beat Plymouth Argyle to temporarily ease relegation fears. Cork continued, 'We always seem to do well during Christmas but to win all four games was extra special. It's all down to hard work. We trained almost every day and it was quite tiring, but it's all been worthwhile.'

Even though WBA had been at the wrong end of the table for an extended period, Atkinson knew the importance of a good run in the FA Cup, having won the competition in 1985 when a young Norman Whiteside settled an exhaustive final in extra time with a swerving, dipping shot. In popular WBA fanzine *Fingerpost*, it was doom and gloom before they even made the trip down, 'What is the FA Cup? To a recent Albion supporter, that is the defeat we suffer in early January against a team from a different (usually lower) division; it's also the reason why we have a blank Saturday at the end of January and no midweek games in March and April. And it hurts.'

Bobby Gould, in contrast, appreciated the FA Cup and its distraction from the league. In his notes in the programme he stated, 'During a long hard Football League programme one gets the opportunity, no matter where you are in the four divisions, or even the Vauxhall Conference [today's National League], to forget three points for a win and league positions mean nothing. Neither does five wins on the trot as we have here at Wimbledon. All that is thrown out the window and it is all or nothing. To me that is why the FA Cup is surely the greatest knockout competition in the world.'

It was a blustery day that had the majority of the West Bank faithful tucked under the roof as the occasional shower came down. It was a healthy crowd of just over 7,200 that had to be patient as the Dons got off to a slow start. The opposition were able to put some passes together but lacked that bit of invention, although Dave Beasant had to be alert on the couple of occasions that his goal did seem vulnerable. This allowed Wimbledon to grow into the game then, with half-time and a possible wake-up call approaching, Dennis Wise supplied a cross that John Fashanu glanced into the goal. It was his 16th of a now prolific season. 'The Dons are on the march again!' he told the media after the game. It was a turning point and took all the air out of the Midlanders. Wise went on a run and let fly a shot from fully 30 yards that flew into the goal, and at 2-0 there was little chance of a fightback as visiting heads went down. 'Steer clear of Plough Lane! No one wants to come here,' Atkinson was quick to tell reporters. 'Everyone will be hoping to avoid Wimbledon, they are so unpredictable. We gave Wimbledon as much of a fright as any team that visited Plough Lane this season but got nothing to show for it.'

Andy Thorn had gained a yellow card in the first half for an industrial challenge that harked back a few weeks prior to the public call from Gould to calm things down a bit. He was the only player to be carded, and it was something that Vinnie Jones was proud of. Once the main instigator of midfield mayhem, even he knew the difference keeping a cooler head was making. 'Don Howe's coaching has made all the difference to me. I've had to prove to him that he's not wasting his time with me. I want to reach even higher standards and, with the club at an all-time high, I can do that. All that time and energy we were wasting is now going into our football.' Jones was even giving advice to a frustrated David Burrows, who had already been booked, but was still careless in his tackles, telling him to 'calm down or you'll get yourself sent off'.

Wise was injured scoring his goal and made way for Robbie Turner. It wasn't long before the new striker found the net with his first goal for the club. 'We came with an open mind, thinking we had a chance, but we never took advantage when we had the wind behind us and a few bits of bad luck cost us the game,' said the Baggies' Don Goodman. Thorn added an own goal five minutes from time to his booking, and subsequent suspension, though the dominant second half was completed with a Carlton Fairweather goal. A final score of 4-1 was lopsided and flattered Wimbledon a little, but once in front the result of the tie never looked in doubt. The next edition of *Fingerpost* wrote, 'The FA Cup is one away match which the club lose. Only last month it happened again. The draw was kind, selecting a First Division power where defeat was expected. In the event, defeat could have been avoided had Williamson put his early chance away, but he didn't, and it wasn't.'

When the draw for the fourth round was made it put the Dons away at Mansfield Town of the Third Division just three weeks later. The Stags had beaten Conference side Bath City 4-0, so this looked like more of a test than the higher placed opposition had just given them.

The Dons were boosted with the return of Terry Gibson to training, but he was still some way off a full return after a hernia operation. John Gannon replaced Wise in attack for the visit of Watford, and the chance to avenge the opening-day defeat. The fixture turned out to be a double blow, however, as a defeat, and a fractured leg suffered by Fairweather, put another cloud into the already grey sky over Plough Lane. Watford had been struggling under Dave Bassett and the former Dons boss didn't get a hero's welcome back as he had already been relieved of his post with the Hornets bottom of the league. It was a game of miscues and errors that was goalless when the half-time tea was brewed. Shortly after the game got back under way, Terry Phelan got the last touch to an effort by Worrel Sterling, although the goal was credited to the Watford midfielder and the visitors were in front. With Thorn out the centre-back pairing of Young and Gayle didn't seem as cohesive but when the former rose highest to power in a header and level on the hour, the unbeaten run looked to be safe. Then the most contentious moment of the game occurred when Luther Blissett ran at Young with the game entering the final ten minutes. The two tangled and it looked like Young was fouled but play kept going and then the defender upended Blissett. A penalty was awarded, when replays would later show the incident was outside the area, and Malcolm Allen hit the winner. Too many players had an off-day for Wimbledon, and they couldn't pick themselves up for the Simod Cup tie away at Coventry just a few days later. The game was played on a very heavy pitch which did more favours in promoting the use of sand than lend itself to any attempt at decent football. Turner got the Dons' goal as they exited the lesser-ranked competition 2-1, with a returning Wally Downes coming in for the stricken Fairweather.

It was amazing that Wimbledon had the run they did, and were in the league position they were in. The treatment room as always was full of aches and breaks, the latest of which was Fairweather's broken leg. The winger didn't even realise the full extent of his injury at first, and only had a full x-ray two days after hobbling off against Watford. When the scan pictures showed the break it was obvious that he would play no further part in the season on the pitch, but being a firm favourite around the training ground and changing room he would still be in the background during his rehabilitation. On the long road back from such an injury he could lean on the experience of Alan Cork, who also broke a leg and was out for almost 18 months, but had returned to be a regular and was banging in the goals. This kind of inspiration would help Fairweather on his way back.

The next scheduled match against Everton was postponed, which allowed extra time for Gould and Howe to prepare for the trip to Field Mill. This was more like it. A proper blood-and-thunder cup tie played on a muddy pitch where the markings were barely visible, and with the crowd tightly packed in the stands. It was a throwback to how the Dons would treat visitors and revel in the chaos when they marched up the leagues and created their own upsets. The fourth round of the FA Cup was still a stage where big upsets could happen, and the form guide showed this was to be considered a banana skin. 'We have no illusions about the task which faces us this afternoon,' Stags manager Ian Greaves said in his notes before the game, 'but believe, that if we are at our best, we can pull off another Mansfield Town giant-killing act. What you can be absolutely certain of is that no effort has been spared with this aim in mind.'

Mansfield had found some form since the turn of the year and had also been scoring plenty of goals in the FA Cup. After a draw in the first round they beat Preston North End 4-2, then beat Lincoln City 4-3, before getting another four when they brushed aside Bath. So, it was no wonder a crowd of just shy of 10,500 was loud before kick-off. With a heavy wind behind them it was the hosts who had most of the play but they couldn't create any real openings. Beasant was equal to their only chance, when Kevin Kent tore on to a back-pass only for the big keeper to save. It was also a quiet afternoon for Fashanu, who was guarded closely by teenage defender Simon Coleman, but a deft touch on one of a couple of occasions that he did get free almost led to a first goal. Phelan ran on to his flick-on and pushed the ball square for Cork, but his shot at goal was cleared off the line by Paul Garner. Just as in the round before a critical blow landed right before half-time. Wise, back in the side but far from 100 per cent fit, did what he always did best and curled over a wicked cross which Cork met at the near post, and the ball was in the top corner.

Usually this would knock the stuffing out of teams, but Mansfield were coming forward and at the same time were still keeping Fashanu quiet, a key part of their game plan that they executed brilliantly, although the same couldn't be said of their finishing. With John Scales at the back Phelan was able to play a more advanced role, and he lodged his first Wimbledon goal. A poor back-pass after a Beasant long punt was quickly seized upon and when Kevin Hitchcock advanced from his goal, Phelan knocked the ball past him as if it were second nature. He jubilantly recalled, 'It was a sweet goal, slotted in at the near post. I don't score that many, and that one was good. I was playing on the left wing. Bobby wanted to try something new. He wanted to take the game to them. I had played there as a kid, but not since. It was a big risk, but I'm like any full-back, you just want to get forward when you get the chance. It was great. Mansfield started quite well while we were a bit shaky, but we got our game together eventually.' At 2-0 the Dons could be forgiven for thinking that it was game over, but a rush of blood to the head and an air kick from Beasant allowed Kent to score into an empty net, and it was game back on. A few minutes later, the home crowd were ecstatic as Sanchez fouled Tony Lowery in the box and a penalty was awarded.

'That was lucky 13. It was the 13th penalty against us this season and only the second Dave has stopped,' Gould beamed afterwards. The game was finely poised when Steve Charles stepped forward to take the kick with 15 minutes left. 'I knew which way he would put the ball,' said Beasant. 'I'd seen him score a penalty on television when Mansfield's Freight Rover Trophy win at Wembley was shown at lunchtime.' This, though, even though Beasant did guess right, was a case of mistaken identity, as Charles explains, 'He dived the right direction, but he got the wrong man. I was not even with Mansfield when they appeared at Wembley!' This was a strange twist of fate, as Beasant saved the kick and his blushes at potentially single-handedly throwing away a two-goal lead in the space of five minutes.

Mansfield were left with a case of what might have been, and captain George Foster couldn't hide his disappointment afterwards, 'If only we could play like this every week, we would be in the top three. There is no reason why we shouldn't.' It seemed strange that this was the type of match that would give belief to a team sitting pretty in the top half in the top division, but Phelan could sense something, 'It had been a hard game. As we travelled back on the coach the feeling grew that this side was destined for Wembley.'

Another strange quirk was that of the FA Cup fifth round draw as out of the hat came Newcastle United, followed by Wimbledon. The two teams were to meet in the league at Plough Lane just two weeks before the cup encounter. It would also mean that by the time the tie rolled around it would be the fourth time the sides had met – not wholly uncommon, but still an oddity. Business was picking up off the field as well with contracts being signed to keep as much of this group of players together as possible. Carlton Fairweather, Lawrie Sanchez, Dennis Wise, Andy Thorn and John Fashanu all committed to another two years. 'I am not worth £1m so stop these transfer stories,' Fash commented when the constant rumours wouldn't stop. 'I am getting tired of all this speculation about my future.'

With the FA Cup now in everyone's thoughts, the bread and butter of the league was starting to play second fiddle, or at least that's what results were showing. The third match of the year against Newcastle was a goalless affair, both teams putting their best poker faces on before locking horns again in the more important meeting a fortnight later. Over 10,000 were in Plough Lane for the First Division encounter, their headline acts of Paul Gascoigne and Mirandinha proving a good enough draw for the neutrals. The game was keenly contested, and what few chances arrived were either rushed, cleared or saved, but kept the crowd interested.

A bright note was the return of Terry Gibson after almost three months out, and he didn't have to wait long before getting among the goals again as in the trip to Selhurst Park to play Charlton Athletic seven days later, he got the equaliser in a 1-1 draw. It was a feisty meeting that saw the team lose their way a bit and would have been steadier if an overhead kick by Wise had gone in instead of hitting a post.

As the game wore on the 'home' side – Charlton were sharing with Crystal Palace at the time – started to believe in themselves more, and Robert Lee drew a foul from Phelan inside the box, and this time Beasant couldn't keep the kick out, Mark Reid successfully beating the captain. The Dons saw their own penalty shout turned down, and then with the rain lashing down Jones hit the woodwork before Gibson netted. He said, 'I was very pleased to get that goal. It ended a nightmare for me because I came to the club to play first-team football and found myself out for 14 weeks. During that time, I felt I had let the club down and now I'm determined to make up for lost time. The directors found a lot of money for my fee and the manager showed a lot of faith when he signed me. The game against Charlton was pretty stormy, it was fortunate that no one was sent off, but the conditions were awkward and that was the cause of some of the problems. It was a very hard game, but I was pleased to get the important goal.'

With Gibson back in the team, and scoring immediately, Gould was more than pleased with his big signing, who he had to personally suffer for. Still with an eye for cover in the squad, and some extra creativity, the manager made one of the club's greatest transfer coups. With the likes of Manchester United and Real Madrid on his CV, and international caps for England, there were eyebrows raised when 31-year-old Laurie Cunningham joined the Dons as a non-contract player. There was no doubt about his ability even as he was coming towards the end of his career. This addition was just the bounce needed as Wimbledon entered the final stretch of the season, and with a date at St James' Park in the diary.

Six

Geordies and Hornets

ONCE IN a while you have a period of games in which you have a team's number. It just works that way and for whatever reason you just can't lose to them, home or away. Even if they have one of the country's most exciting emerging talents for many years in their ranks. And a big money Brazilian. Newcastle United just couldn't beat Wimbledon in 1987/88, and when the biggest game of their four meetings came, they became more and more frustrated. 'Two weeks ago, we met the Dons for the third time this season,' manager Willie McFaul opened in the matchday programme, 'and I thought we earned our point. But the fact remains that we have played them three times this season and still haven't come out on top. They deserved to beat us here in September, but the result that really hurt us was their Littlewoods Cup victory at Plough Lane in October. You only have to look at Wimbledon's results this season and last to appreciate what a difficult side they are to beat. We will have to hit top form today if we are to make our home advantage count.'

'We went up on the Friday morning. We got into the hotel then did a bit of training,' Andy Thorn recalled. The team were staying in the same hotel as some members of the press so they relaxed with them in the evening, just a small 'session' according to the defender. Newcastle had beaten Crystal Palace and Swindon Town so far without conceding a goal, 1-0 and 5-0 respectively, and had only lost one game since the turn of the year, a 3-1 reverse the week before to Norwich City. With the FA Cup form goes out the window though, and as the rounds go on and Wembley comes more into view, fortune favours the brave. Bobby Gould was brave and set his team out to win the tie and proof of that was when he gave Laurie Cunningham his debut. The back four were settled now with Brian Gayle and Thorn renewing their partnership at the heart of defence, and Clive Goodyear was getting a lengthy run in the team, ever present since early December, with Terry Phelan on the other side. John Fashanu and Terry Gibson kept Alan Cork on the bench, and Dennis Wise, Lawrie Sanchez and Vinnie Jones joined the new boy in midfield.

This was core Wimbledon.

The skilful players of Newcastle had to resort to physicality, but most of it was after the game when tempers frayed, and otherwise cool heads boiled over. Mirandinha was the main culprit for nearly causing a riot following the final whistle. It took just six minutes for the first goal. Glenn Roeder fouled Fashanu, Wise provided another accurate cross, and the smallest player on the pitch headed in at the near post. 'It was a difficult tie on paper, but we took our chances well,' Gibson said later. 'A lot of defenders find it hard to cope with a shorter player because they have to stoop down when they make a challenge. It paid off because I got enough space to head home the goal.'

The goal being so early gave Newcastle time to regroup and they had the better chances, passing up some good opportunities to draw level. Paul Gascoigne, Darren Jackson and Paul Goddard were all left wondering how they missed. 'It was a big year for me personally, thanks to the help of Don Howe's coaching. I won my first England under-21 cap, and that extra experience helped me deal with the likes of Gascoigne and Mirandinha,' said Thorn, who was instrumental in keeping Newcastle's attacking qualities limited. To punish their woeful finishing, the Dons showed them how it was done with another set-piece goal, Wise again floating over a devilish ball which Gayle was obliged to head home. But the two-goal lead was halved inside two minutes as Neil McDonald met Gascoigne's corner, his effort taking a heavy touch off Cork – who had replaced Cunningham – to get his team back into the game. This set up a frantic last half an hour, and the Dons to their credit withstood the pressure. A few minutes from the end

Fashanu sent up a speculative lob which caught out Gary Kelly to seal the tie and put Wimbledon into the quarter-finals for the second straight season.

'I know I have a side which can go anywhere and give any team a good game,' Gould said proudly. 'A wonderful bunch of lads. We are the biggest party spoilers that football has seen in the past ten years. They have tremendous inner strength and are a wonderful set of individuals who play well together.' This was a big win for Wimbledon and even though they were the Toon's bogey team, they did a great job of handling the pressure and didn't rise to the hostile atmosphere. Gibson saw it as a breakthrough too, 'We had hoped to keep it 0-0 for a while to quieten the fans down so going ahead after just six minutes was important. It's great for me to be back in the big time and I hope now we can go all the way to Wembley. I've never got into the quarter-finals of the FA Cup before.'

Wimbledon were on their way to Wembley.

This wasn't an early advance warning or rally cry; they had qualified for the Mercantile Credit Centenary Festival tournament. For the first time in 25 years they would play at the old stadium and it could well be a preview as to what they could achieve now they were in the last eight of the FA Cup. The 16 teams competing over the weekend gained their place through their form over a 15-game period. Everton, Manchester United, Luton Town, Nottingham Forest, Sheffield Wednesday and Liverpool had also qualified from the First Division, along with four teams from the Second Division – Aston Villa, Leeds United, Blackburn Rovers and Crystal Palace. They were joined by Sunderland and Wigan Athletic from the Third Division, with the Fourth Division represented by Wolverhampton Wanderers and Tranmere Rovers. It was encouraged that all clubs send their first teams. The draw was kind for the Dons as they had the lowest-ranked team in the tournament in the first round, Tranmere, in the very first match of the weekend. The rest of the draw had been made as well, and should the Dons progress, they would face a quarter-final against Liverpool or Newcastle United. There was definitely a smell of fate in the air.

Football has a strange but all too common way of bringing you back down to earth with a hefty bump, and so when the team went to Loftus Road to take on a Queens Park Rangers team who had fallen out of the title race but were still looking down on Wimbledon in the table, they had a wake-up call. The 1-0 scoreline was just about all the game deserved and even the silky play of Laurie Cunningham could not light up a very dull match. The plastic pitch was something that Wimbledon struggled on, and inside the last ten minutes it seemed a drab goalless draw was the outcome that matched the display from both sets of players. Then John Byrne scrambled home a corner to snatch the points for Rangers. It wasn't often that the Dons let themselves and the fans down, and after the euphoric scenes up at Tyneside they just couldn't lift themselves enough off the artificial surface to make any impression on the game. They were also without Dennis Wise, who had been instrumental in the majority of goals scored. Luckily, their next opponents were also punching above their weight. Luton Town had reached Wembley, not just for the Mercantile Credit tournament but also for the League Cup Final. In a similar mould they were taking on the big teams and getting credible results, and with Wimbledon's own lofty ambitions of reaching a Wembley final it was a good test, at just the right time.

As part of the preparations for the upcoming games, and reward for the success in the FA Cup so far, Bobby Gould had arranged to take his team away to Spain for some training and team time. The destination was Estepona, and as Dave Beasant explained, it was good to get away: 'The week away gave us a change of environment. Our training ground was getting very boggy, but we didn't have too much luck with the weather in Spain because it rained for a couple of days.' The best-laid plans and intentions sometimes go awry, but you could sense this was vital for the final run-in, as Beasant continued, 'It was worthwhile though because it gave us a chance to get back to the way we've been brought up, as a close-knit family. But now we've got to make it worthwhile for the club, by getting into the semi-final of the FA Cup.'

First though, Luton were in town, and after the week in the sun (and rain) the manager rearranged his attacking line with Wise still out, and so the unfamiliar sight of John Scales in the number 11 shirt appeared in the warm-ups, but he was to be at left-back with Phelan pushed forward again just as he had been successfully deployed at Mansfield. Luton seemed otherwise distracted with a semi-final three days later against Swindon in the Simod Cup, and their own FA Cup quarter-final with Portsmouth. Their former England international defender Steve Foster was on the bench after surgery and other regulars were missing from their line-up. The usual suspects got the two goals – Fashanu just after ten minutes and Gibson shortly after half-time.

'Fergie [Alex Ferguson] called me Dick Turpin. He accused me of going north and of highway robbery when I got Gibbo for that price,' Gould laughed as the £200,000 fee for Gibson was increasingly looking like a steal. 'It was a real snip at that money and Gibbo is proving it now. Three years ago I told Dave Bassett he should buy Terry.'

The partnership beginning to flourish with Fashanu was no surprise, but what was though, was the midfield play of Vinnie Jones, who was the supplier of both goals. 'It was a victory for us and one which puts us back in contention with the teams chasing Liverpool at the top of the table. Now we're in the right frame of mind for our cup tie against Watford,' said Gould, wrapping the afternoon up knowing the biggest game of his tenure at the club was a week away.

Wary of how his players could get too excited ahead of big matches and let their thoughts take over and let them overflow and tumble out of their mouths, Gould slapped a restrictive gagging order on his team in the build-up to the quarter-final. 'When we played Watford in the league a few weeks ago some of our players said things which did not do us any favours,' the manager explained. Gould feared that the team could also trip themselves up and get caught up in the hype, as they had done the previous year when losing to Tottenham, so it was best to be cautious and not let any distractions in. Spurs that day won with two late goals and then went on to face Watford in the last four, so the opposition were also out to match their exploits of a year before and go one better.

In 1983 Laurie Cunningham had to pull out of the FA Cup Final at the very last minute due to injury. His time at Manchester United was cut short due to this, 'I knew I wasn't 100 per cent fit and, although my name was down to play, I didn't feel I could run the risk of letting myself and the team down. It was awful having to miss out on such an occasion, but it was my decision to sit it out, not Ron Atkinson's.' United went on to win the trophy after beating Brighton & Hove Albion in a replay. Back in England after spells abroad, Cunningham was now nearing peak fitness, 'I'm fitter than I've been for two or three years, and I'm determined to prove it with Wimbledon. I also aim to prove I'm not just a winger. I wanted to get rid of that number

11 shirt so people wouldn't continue to class me as "just a winger". I'm an attacking midfield player and that's the role I want to be remembered for.'

Now 31, Cunningham wanted to stay and finish his career in England, 'I got a phone call from John Fashanu asking if I was interested in coming to Plough Lane. It sounded like the opportunity I'd been waiting for. It began as a week-to-week deal designed to give the club a chance to assess me and vice versa. I'm enjoying it here and am keen to stay.' He was given a baptism of fire with the Dons at Newcastle in the FA Cup win, and had seen enough from his new team-mates, 'I think Wimbledon can go all the way to Wembley now. It will be a tough game against Watford, but we must fancy our chances. Having come so close to playing in a cup final for Manchester United I'd love the chance to appear at Wembley in a Wimbledon shirt.'

Wimbledon had not beaten Watford so far in 1987/88, so maybe the Hornets were their kryptonite just like the Dons were to Newcastle. Over 12,000 poured into Plough Lane, not the biggest attendance of the season but almost double the normal average. The supporters had never really created a constant barrage of sound, and the extra tension of this game, with its importance, meant that more nerves were in evidence, creating a low buzz of anticipation.

When Malcolm Allen scored for Newcastle, and Brian Gayle was sent off for striking an opponent in the last incident of the first half, the mood at the break was ghostly quiet – apart from the busy Wandle End of the ground that housed the Watford fans. Did they really have a hoodoo on the Dons? It was time to focus, time for those big hearts to swell again in the big chests. Cork was sacrificed so that the defence could keep its shape, with Eric Young coming on into the middle. The red mist that had descended over Gayle needed to vanish from all the players. The move seemed inspired when Young jumped higher than everyone else to thump a header home just three minutes after the second half started. It was Wise with yet another set-piece delivery after Phelan was fouled by Nigel Gibbs. 'We were always good from dead balls. Something like 84 per cent of our goals came from set pieces and most of them came from Wise. This was no different,' Gould remembered.

The tie was now in the balance, and there was nothing more powerful than a wounded Womble. Watford started to wilt and even though they had an additional man it seemed like they had been reduced to ten men. Fashanu had equalled his best seasonal goal tally of 18 a week before, and he would go on to set a new personal best when reaching 19 against the Hornets with one straight out of his stereotypical best. Bearing down on John McClelland he charged down the attempted clearance, then in a flash he gathered the ball under control and the only person in his way, and a route to the semi-final, was Tony Coton, but there was no denying the £1m-rated man as he calmly slotted the ball past the experienced stopper then stood in front of a delirious terrace with his arms high and wide, team-mates jumping all over him.

Andy Thorn was one of the most relieved during the celebrations. 'I was sick at the time,' he said, as he blamed himself for the Watford goal. 'It was a dream result and proves that we are really a team to be reckoned with now. We were up against it but then we came back superbly and showed everyone that we've got a really good side now. We have got a tendency to take things easy against the smaller teams while we go hammer and tongs against the big teams, but apart from that I think we're doing very well now.' Thorn had to switch to left-back at the break when the changes were made. No other player was left-sided, so he was the best option, 'It wasn't a problem and I quite enjoyed it. When we went 2-1 up, Terry was able to come back to the left position and I finished the game just sweeping up behind the defence.'

Gould knew the Dons had pulled another rabbit out of the hat, 'It was all about the mental strength of the team and the players had it in bucketloads. You had to have it at Wimbledon, or you wouldn't survive. We managed to come back against Watford when the odds were stacked so firmly against us. We were mentally tough as a unit.'

On the same day that Wimbledon booked their historic place in the last four, two other teams made it through. Nottingham Forest beat Arsenal 2-1 at Highbury and Luton swept past Portsmouth 3-1. The following day Liverpool, who were odds-on to win the league, and the double, went to Maine Road and stuck four past Manchester City without conceding. No one wanted Liverpool at this stage, but equally no one wanted Wimbledon.

Four numbered balls clattered around inside a velvet bag for just a minute, and then the draw was complete: Liverpool v Nottingham Forest, and Wimbledon v Luton Town. That feeling of fate.

Tottenham Hotspur would have joined Newcastle in being glad to see the back of the Dons in 1987/88. After losing 3-0 in north London on Halloween, they went down by the same score in south-west London on 19 March. What a difference a year makes as the team who had put an end to Wimbledon's FA Cup adventure in 1987, for all their neat and tidy passing, just rolled over again once Vinnie Jones scored at the midpoint of the second half. Fashanu reached another milestone with his 20th goal of the season, a pinpoint header, and Wise also scored with his head to make the score a little unfair given the balance of play, but where Spurs were toothless up front they got a lesson in finishing again. There was a big blot on the Dons' copybook though as Clive Goodyear left the field with a broken leg, the victim of a rough challenge by Clive Allen. Originally the x-ray wasn't showing an obvious break, but on second viewing there was a small one in his tibia. Although not on the level of Carlton Fairweather's injury, this setback would see the right-back out of action for several weeks on early estimates. One thing was certain – he would be out of the games in April which included trips to both Merseyside teams, and the FA Cup semi-final at White Hart Lane against Luton, his old club.

Liverpool were the next opponents in the league, adding to that feeling of fate. As much as they were the team to beat, and the ones everyone up and down the land envied, their manager remained humble when it came to how Wimbledon had made their way up the leagues. Kenny Dalglish was one of Europe's best players in his prime and would find his way into most First Division teams, 'The critics claimed that the newcomers to the First Division wouldn't be able to live with the kind of competition they would meet. Wimbledon gave their answer by picking up 66 points and finishing sixth from top [in 1986/87]. They have reached the semi-finals of the FA Cup for the first time and, indeed, if things worked out that way, they could be meeting us again at Wembley in May. Having said that though, I'm not tempting fate! I'm not among those who have criticised Wimbledon's style of play, and I'm not going to start now. We play our way, they play theirs, and if the styles contrast, that's no reflection on them. You can anticipate that when Wimbledon are in action, there's always going to be plenty of excitement when it comes to goalmouth incidents.'

Dalglish could have done a good job as a PR man for the Dons. The warm words were extended across Stanley

Park three days later when Wimbledon were entertained by Everton, and their boss Colin Harvey, 'Top marks go to Bobby Gould and the coach Don Howe, for a job well done, and also to the previous manager Dave Bassett for setting the pattern. They have a good set of players who work to a system which suits them. It's different to the way we like to play, but no one should criticise Wimbledon for that. It takes all sorts to make up the English First Division and part of its attraction is that there are different styles.'

Liverpool were setting all kinds of records on their relentless march to the title but had just been beaten 1-0 in the derby, although Everton were way off the pace and would not be a factor down the final stretch. Wimbledon had shocked the Reds on their first visit to Anfield, but this time the roles were reversed as the champions-elect were not firing on all cylinders in the early stages and Gould's men were holding their own until John Aldridge managed to outjump Eric Young to break the deadlock ten minutes before the break with a looping header from a Steve Nicol cross.

Wimbledon were better in the opening minutes of the second half, but despite both Sanchez and Cork going close, they couldn't find a way through and after the Reds weathered the storm, John Barnes sent a low shot past Beasant. Surprisingly, instead of expressing their power, Liverpool were content in playing keep-ball and wasting time, the main culprit being player-manager Dalglish, who introduced himself into the game for his first appearance of the season. Cheers from the home crowd turned to jeers from the visiting fans as he repeatedly took the ball into the corners, or played back-passes with Bruce Grobbelaar. Eric Young, who was fortunate to stay on the pitch after an obvious foul on Peter Beardsley when already on a card, atoned for being beaten for the first goal by scoring one of his own in the last minute. Aldridge remained ahead of Fashanu in the First Division goalscoring table, two clear of the Dons' main marksman. 'I'd love to meet them at Wembley,' the Republic of Ireland international said. 'They deserve their success for the way they have come up from the Southern League. It would be a magic occasion for them to get to Wembley.' Be careful what you wish for, Aldo.

Fashanu had an off-day in so much that he didn't score, but insisted that the result wouldn't have any bearing if the two met again in mid-May. 'We had several key players missing, and some young lads in the side,' he said. Goodyear was replaced by Scales, and Jones missed the game with Vaughan Ryan coming in for his first start in over five months. 'We could even have nicked something in the end. So, we'd be confident enough, whenever and wherever we meet them again,' Fashanu concluded.

John Scales was in at the deep end after being called in to replace Goodyear, but as Wimbledon always proved, the next man up remained ready and willing. The defender said, 'We had a great chance to beat them because they weren't playing at their best, but we didn't capitalise on it. I had been looking forward to playing against John Barnes and it was obviously one of the biggest, if not the biggest, games I've played in. I was happy with the way I played, but like the whole team, I was disappointed at the end because we created as many chances as they did.'

The honours were even at Goodison Park and then again a few days later at The Dell, the games offering up eight goals between them. Everton had stuttered in the defence of a title they won so handsomely 12 months previously, but against the Dons it was clear why they had fallen from their perch. Laurie Cunningham scored his first goal for the club, a well-taken chance following Fashanu's cross with just two minutes on the clock, and the visitors should have put the game to bed early but Young put his header over. They paid the penalty, literally, when Trevor Steven converted from the spot and then Neil Pointon gave the Toffees the lead with 20 minutes played. Wise soon levelled and what had started as an entertaining game fizzled out. In a throwback to days not so long ago, Vinnie Jones saw red after kicking Peter Reid while the England player was on the ground. Jones was only just back from suspension and now another was due. Reduced to ten men, the Dons sat back and protected the point gained.

At Southampton it was two substitutes who rescued a hard-fought point as Brian Gayle and Andy Clement combined to earn another 2-2 draw. Cunningham scored again, a habit that would be very welcome and something that the player he was covering for, Fairweather, was often used to doing. It was another goal produced by Fashanu, proving his value not just in scoring, his headed pass over John Burridge allowing the former Real Madrid star to score into an unguarded net. Lawrie Sanchez had to leave the game, another man ending up in Steve Allen's busy treatment room after he was hacked at by Glenn Cockerill. The Saints got back in the game when Ryan wildly sliced a clearance and Graham Baker headed in. Eight minutes from time Cockerill, the pantomime villain of their team, scored what looked to be the wining goal, but with Gayle pushed into an emergency forward position the Dons found a way through when Clement, on for Cork, pulled the ball back for the makeshift centre-forward to grab a point.

There was one more match to go before the latest biggest day of the Wimbledon fairy tale, and this was more a horror story as Coventry remained unbeaten against the Dons that season. The game made headlines for the wrong reasons as some saw the early departure of John Fashanu as gamesmanship ahead of the White Hart Lane clash. His 'injury' was seen by some in the written media as a smokescreen, but Wimbledon had already fielded a weakened team, giving a debut to Paul Miller, while Clement and Ryan were in a midfield that looked far from robust, and even though Jones was back it didn't have that imposing feel. Wimbledon played within themselves and it showed, conceding twice in a minute halfway through the first half. The FA Cup holders had not backed up that epic win over Tottenham and were a comfortable mid-table side. Terry Phelan played goalkeeper for a moment when he handled a David Phillips shot, and Brian Kilcline tucked away the penalty. Seconds later the Sky Blues' Wembley hero Keith Houchen made it two. Young, with an uncanny knack for scoring, did just that before the half ended to make it 2-1, and despite some huff and puff the Dons couldn't blow down the Coventry door.

The Striker's Story
Terry Gibson

TERRY GIBSON was Spurs through and through, 'Tottenham Hotspur was my team. I grew up as a kid supporting them. I had chances to join other clubs all over the country, and I could have gone to Anderlecht in Belgium. I was training with them for a couple of years during school holidays, but Spurs was always the club I set my heart on joining. At the age of 14 I signed schoolboy forms, and at 16 an apprenticeship. Within a few months of leaving school I played in the first team. It was a dream, incredible.'

It was every schoolboy's dream, in fact. 'I was standing on the terraces, and a few months later playing in a game against Stoke City, then two against Manchester United at home in the FA Cup, then the replay three days later up at Old Trafford.' Quite the introduction. 'My first game I was 17 years and six days old, you're suddenly playing with your heroes. Months before that I was getting their autographs, then I'm playing in the same team as them. All of a sudden, you've gone from a fan, into a changing room, playing, being picked, and sitting on the team bus. It was the time of my life to be honest. I played three games as a 17-year-old, then 20 in the last year of my contract. I scored seven or eight goals, and then my contract was up. I wasn't happy with the new terms offered, which was a one-year deal with a £15-a-week rise. Take it or leave it.'

Gibson was frustrated, feeling that his efforts deserved more, 'I'd played the last 20 games of the season; I was on a four-year deal when I was 17. Keith Burkinshaw said he wanted younger players to be kept on their toes [and] not to get too comfortable, but I didn't see it like that. There was no negotiations, it was a letter in the post that you had to reply to by letter, and my answer was I don't accept these terms. This was back in the day when you didn't have freedom of contract, so you had to suffer the consequences, which meant in theory I could have been there another three years on the same terms I was on, and they could release you at the drop of a hat. It was terrible when you think back now. Your contract was up but you still were tied to that club until they got money for you. So, fortunately in my case it was resolved pretty quickly as Coventry City came in for me. Bobby Gould was the manager. I was trying to leave Tottenham and I played in a pre-season game, we won 6-4 down at Lewes and I scored five. Gould's brother was manager of Lewes and told Bobby that I'd scored five, and he was interested in me anyway, so on the Monday morning he put a bid in of £75,000 and it was accepted. I went to Coventry, and worked with Bob for the first time,'

Most people will know Gibson from his time at Highfield Road, which was where he started to flourish and get among the goals. It wasn't all plain sailing though, 'I had two and a half years there, and from about six months in I felt I didn't think I was going to be at the club long. Because nobody was. Bobby was manager, and at that time he was under pressure for his job. I think in my two and a half years there we had three different chairmen. Players were coming and going. I signed for the club, and we were literally signing players on the day of games. Micky Gynn signed and played at Watford in the first game of the season. He met us at Vicarage Road, we'd never met him before, he played had a blinder. We won with about eight new players. It always seemed a place, Coventry, where managers and players would come and go, and because of that I never really felt that I'd be settled.'

The unnerving feeling was something that formed part of the football business which Terry was learning quickly. 'The club was always looking to sell players if they could make a profit. I scored quite a few goals, 19 in each of my first two seasons, then 14 by January. No one kept league or cup goals, it was just a total, so I always remember my totals, so I couldn't tell you the competition split. It really hacked me off I didn't get to 20, so that's why I can remember them easily. I was on course for my best season at Christmas, and then went to Manchester United. Coventry was great though. It was a really forward-thinking football club in the fact it had underground pitch heating, an all-seater stadium, electric scoreboard. No one else had any of those, I think Arsenal had the soil heating, but no one else had all-seater. We had a magnificent training ground, but it was just a place that was a stop-off really, for players and managers. As I said we had three chairmen in my time, which was ridiculous, and it hasn't changed, they're still having the same problems.'

Manchester United. Old Trafford, the Theatre of Dreams; United were going through a lean phase and boss Ron Atkinson was soon to leave his post, making Gibson one of his last signings. 'Eighteen months at United. I joined in the January, and I was flying. I was really confident, but I had to wait a year until I started a game at home, so the wheels completely came off. I went there full of optimism and confidence, and I made two starts, one in January, and one at the end of the season, Liverpool and Newcastle. Then I started against Leicester City at the early part of the next season but had to wait until January to start another game. Against Arsenal, we won 2-0, and I scored my only goal for United. By that stage I'd pretty much made my mind up that I was going to be leaving, and go play first-team football somewhere regularly again.'

United were in their transition phase and Alex Ferguson was at the helm after replacing Atkinson. 'He [Ferguson] was great. He gave me an opportunity with more games, but it was just weird as I lost all confidence so quickly. You go there and you think you might not be first choice as there was other good strikers there.' Gibson wasn't against healthy competition and had attributes others didn't. 'I always felt I was different to the others that were at the club. They were all big, strong, could play with their back to goal. I was the one that could run in behind, I was the quickest, and I'd scored more goals that season than any of the United strikers, but just never got the opportunity. When that keeps happening week in, week out, you're on the bench or in the stand, you lose confidence. I was in my early 20s, looking back now you think, "Why did he [Atkinson] buy me? He clearly don't rate me." In fact he tried to loan me out back to Coventry pretty soon after I got there. It was confusing.'

The sense of irony wasn't lost on Gibson as the season would end with both his former clubs getting to Wembley for the FA Cup Final and along the way one would eliminate his United team. 'Coventry knocked us out, and I played in the game at Old Trafford. It was in a period that I was getting games under Fergie. I think it was after the Arsenal game, we beat them in a big result and people still talk about the game. David Rocastle was sent off, Norman Whiteside and I should have got sent off about three times each! It was the first Arsenal–United battle. People remember the Wenger–Ferguson ones, but the supporters really do recall that one, George Graham and Fergie, and a week later we played Coventry, and got beat. It was a farce of a game as one half of the pitch, one end to the other was frozen solid, and the other soft. So from penalty spot to penalty spot, right down the middle it was two different surfaces. If you went on one side with the wrong footwear on you couldn't stand up and vice versa. When I left Coventry, we never got past the third or fourth round so there was never any real hope of a cup run or winning it.' It was with a laugh Gibson recalled the situation, 'I leave and within a year they're knocking us out at Old Trafford, and go on and win it, and it was against Spurs, my other old team! Now I'm desperate to leave United and watching the two teams I just left battle it out in the FA Cup Final.'

Rewinding back a bit further to what could have been, Gibson said, 'I was at Tottenham when they won the cup in the early 80s. I wasn't in the team or in the squad, but I was around the club. Steve Archibald, Garth Crooks, Glenn Hoddle, Ricky Villa; I was only 19 and I wasn't involved, but it gave me that ambition of playing in the final. Two years on the trot when they're involved making their records and doing all the other stuff in the build-up [to the 1981 and 1982 finals]. "I've got to play in one," I thought, after Coventry beat Spurs and I'm stuck at United thinking is this the end of my career, thoroughly depressed, thinking it's never going to happen. Initially from Coventry I could have gone back to Tottenham, they wanted me back. Burkinshaw had left, and Peter Shreeves had become manager. He was my reserve and youth team manager but the club wouldn't pay £300,000.

Having sold me for £70,000 they were reluctant to pay what United were going to pay.'

The time had come to leave Manchester, but no one was putting any bids in. 'I had a big bust-up with Fergie, I'd moved out and sold my house in Manchester, and I was living in a crumby hotel in there, waiting for someone to come and buy me with no real indication that was going to happen. To be honest I was just thinking it was the end, then out the blue Bobby Gould got the Wimbledon job and one of his first calls was to track me down and see if I'd be interested in going to the Dons. The main attraction to be honest was Bob because I'd played well for him at Coventry. I knew he believed in me, and that's what I desperately needed. He said, "I'll deal with it." So I went into Fergie the next day and I said, "Has anyone come in for me?" and he said "no". I tried again. "Tell me," I said. "Have you spoken to Bobby Gould?" Again he said no, then I said, "Swear on your daughter's life." "No, I can't do that, tell him I want £200,000 and you can go," so I literally went downstairs from Fergie's office, used the payphone in the training ground to ring Gouldy back and told him. Literally half an hour later I was packing up my stuff and heading back to London.'

At last Gibson was out of the torrid time at United, which should have been one of his best career moves, although he had nothing but praise for his now former boss, 'Fergie was great. He knew my situation, he'd just joined the club, and he wanted new players. I kept seeing names linked with the club, Brian McClair, Mark Hughes was coming back, the last thing I wanted to be doing was sitting behind Frank Stapleton, Peter Davenport and those two. So it was clear he wanted some in, and some had to go, so he was quite happy for me to go. He was happy for me to stay; he didn't push me out, we got on. He totally had respect for Wimbledon. It was always fun [against United], there was always a punch-up. He hated the way we went about the game, but I think as the years went on it was clear that he respected the managers that we had, and that we had a small budget and facilities. He didn't like some of our players and the way we played, but we always caused them trouble, and other big clubs. He was a manager I got on with. After I left, I kept a decent relationship with him at the time, and when I was with Lawrie [Sanchez] at Wycombe I would ring him up and ask if we could use their training ground and he was happy to do so, he was never an issue.'

Life at Wimbledon was always going to be different, and the club was going through changes under new management, but Gibson had his own issues to deal with which would hamper his progress. 'Most of my seasons at Wimbledon were blighted by injury and that first year was in particular. I had a hernia then in rehabilitation to get over that, I did the other side. It was common then, so it was two ops in my first season. The second hernia one was put off until the Tuesday after the cup final. I tore the first, and had the op. I knew I'd done the second, but we agreed at the club that I would get through and play somehow. Don't do an awful lot and certain types of training and not the normal set. The agreement we all came to was until we got knocked out the cup as we fancied our chances in it, and we waited until then to have the second op. My injury record at the Dons was poor, but I never missed a game because of little injuries. It was a broken ankle, two on my groin, I snapped a hamstring off the bone, and I broke my wrist after eight months out with an ankle injury, and then a bad operation on that pinned and screwed. My first training session back someone had had a shot which deflected and hit my arm and broke my wrist.' It really was amazing that Gibson had any game time at all, let alone managed to score goals. 'So again, we agreed that we'd go in plaster for six weeks and play with a broken wrist until the end of the season. But the bone died, so I had to have a bone graft, and

I missed the first three months of the next season. I've got a big scar on my hip from the graft, so I never just had a little injury.'

The Crazy Gang style and attitude meant you had to suffer a little to get to the top. 'It was part and parcel of playing for Wimbledon. The way we played took its toll to be honest. It was hard work. We trained harder than any other team I'd played at, harder than we probably should have looking back now. I mean, there's no fun in playing on Saturday, no rehab on Sunday, come in Monday and do a ten-mile run and then an 11v11 for an hour. It was killing us. We were fit and stronger than others, but I never had that feeling of sharpness that I had at other clubs where I'd trained in a more realistic, sensible manner. It was about how far could you be pushed at the Dons, with all the managers, and it took its toll on my body.'

Wimbledon were defying the critics again, but Gibson and other signings that were made in the summer were still trying to fully integrate into the Crazy Gang fold. It was an exclusive set of players that made the club unique, but one game changed the thinking. 'It was a real coming together and really pivotal to what we did that year. Up until that point we had half new, half old players, and there wasn't a real acceptance of the new from the old.

Then going to Newcastle in the cup [changed that]. Vinnie had alleged death threats and the grabbing Gazza incident, they were out for blood, and had a good team. It was a packed house there; you forget how many people you'd get on football terraces. So the pressure was on, and we were brilliant. On the journey back we went by train, and I remember looking and for the first time it was all of us together. Instead of the old and new split, there was that element but not everybody. The older ones were still taking to Bob and Don, and they were not sure if they trusted us to do the same as what they'd done. They'd lost their mates to Watford and Sheffield United, other clubs, and Harry [Bassett] had left so that Newcastle trip, working as a team and achieving it together, what we did in that game and the journey home all of a sudden there wasn't this divide.'

The next round was the moment that Wimbledon began to believe an FA Cup win was possible. 'Watford in the quarter-finals, that's a game we fancy ourselves in, and then who knows after that. Corky got taken off, and Young came on,' Gibson recalled of the changes made following Brian Gayle's red card. 'Gayley never got his place back. Eric was one of the first-year players at the club and from then on, he never looked back, so that was also a turning point. Going 1-0 down never phased us, down to ten men never phased us, and in that game even though in that period you think "oh shit", we rallied around, made the changes at half-time, and I never had any doubt at the end to at least come back and stay in the cup. It was big to come back in those circumstances, you're getting closer as the run goes on, we had to dig deep, but it didn't surprise me when we did it.'

The semi-finals were up next and the circle was complete for Gibson as it meant a return to White Hart Lane, where it had all started. 'We drove in our own cars and parked where we could around the ground; we wanted to keep the same format. We both avoided the other two in the draw which was what we wanted to do and at that stage both teams are thinking it's the draw we wanted.' Wimbledon and Luton had missed the big guns of Liverpool and Nottingham Forest in the draw. 'Nerves play a big part. You're so anxious to do well and a bit of fear creeps in because you're so close to getting to the final. We're talking about a competition back then that meant so much. My dream, my ambition, to play in the cup final and you're that close. The semi-finals were not at Wembley then, so you had fewer chances to get there. Once we had nothing to lose and we had to fight back I thought we fully deserved the win in the end. I got fouled for the penalty, Fash slotted it home coolly under the circumstances. Would he take it in the same manner as all his penalties? But he did and that helped us, and then I came off, my race was run because of my groin. Then a decent goal from a throw-in out on the right. Crossed in and Wise two-footed it in like a tackle. I can't put into words what it felt like. It was a relief that we don't look back now and have that heartbreak of getting beat in the semi. Then reality set in, "Oh god, we're playing Liverpool.'"

After getting to the final there was still quite a few games to play in the league. Gibson had his own issues with injuries but could sense that others were a little guarded going into those matches, fearing getting injured themselves. 'Carlton Fairweather, who was an important member of the team, had broken his leg, so we'd all had a warning, and he was going to miss the final so we were all aware that each one of us in a small squad were at risk of picking up an injury. I don't think there was a shutdown or anything as we finished seventh in the league. If we hadn't had the run, we could have finished top four. To be honest were we massive underdogs? Not really. Yes, we were underdogs because of the size of the club's fanbase, wage bill, transfer fees and stuff, but in terms of our season, if we hadn't been in the cup, we might have finished a lot closer to them than people imagine.'

Gibson and the team weren't kidding themselves about the size of their task, but they were far from fearful of it, 'There was always a belief there that we can not just give them a game, but we can win this. Why did we think that, as they were so good, so big, had all the star players? But we still had belief that we could win. That was the spirit of the club and players. We loved the challenge, the bigger the better. The first-year players all bought into it, you couldn't help buying into it. Every year we had the lowest budget but still got promotion, they worked their way through the leagues, and now in the final why would we change and go there and think, "Let's just hope we don't get beat by too much," so we went there thinking we could beat them. We knew what they were and weren't good at. We can cause them problems, we were good defensively, and we work hard. We know what we're doing and we're tasty at set pieces and they are awful at defending them, so if we get half a dozen decent ones that's three or four chances for us to score, that was our game plan. Houghton and Beardsley told me since they never practised against them as they thought they were so good at everything else they wouldn't need to.

They'd beat us in open play, and we wouldn't even get too many free kicks and corners. We spent three hours on ours the night before.'

The night and morning before the final was something that Gibson thought was a normal Wimbledon away day, only with a few more cameras about, 'We had our own private restaurant in the hotel. We noticed Gouldy was being interviewed by Bob Wilson out on the patio, and we were on the first floor. We all started chucking bread rolls at them out the window. I remember Wisey ordered loads of ketchup as he liked it on everything, even his spaghetti bolognese would be smothered in it! We were used to staying in small hotels back then and Gouldy was scared we'd get thrown out the Cannizaro Hotel so he came up and said, "Can't you all clear off down the pub or something, go and cause havoc down there," so Corky said, "You wouldn't dare." Bob said "it won't hurt to have a walk", and Corky said, "Put your hand in your pocket a buy a round," so Bob gave him some cash. I'm not sure how much and Corky's never told us.

'We all walked down the pub about 9pm on a lovely summer evening. No one recognised us – 15, 20 people in there, but no one said, "Oh, that's the Dons." It didn't seem to capture the imagination of the public in that part of Wimbledon, in the

Village. No one got drunk, most of us didn't have a drink, some had a beer, one max, and we all walked back. All you could hear that night before the biggest game of our lives was laughter from all the rooms. It kind of felt like we were on a jolly boys' outing like *Only Fools and Horses*, but we were all on a lads' weekend away playing in the cup final. It was a masterstroke as if we'd stayed in the hotel in our rooms and sitting there thinking about the game we'd have drove ourselves mad and that's when the fear and doubt can creep in. It was good camaraderie.' Nothing more than you'd expect from the quiet nature of the team.

'It was all very emotional,' Terry said as the day finally arrived. 'We had the build-up during the week, we made the record at Abbey Road, we did the press day. It was big news, and because it was Wimbledon v Liverpool, such a contrast, and just us being in it was a massive story. Cameras all around the hotel, me and Clive were getting ready, and there's a camera looking through the window! It was on TV. We were putting our suits on and watching us on TV! Then cameras on the bus, on the helicopter above the bus, it was incredible. You go out on the pitch doing interviews and barely hear a word of what questions are being asked to you, and you're trying to take it in. My former team-mates at

United, who we played the Monday before, telling me make sure you take it in and enjoy it. We had Gordon Strachan, Arthur Albiston, Bryan Robson, wishing us good luck just after they'd kicked us off the pitch! So you try and take it in, and at the same time you think "this is as good as it gets", so I found it quite emotional. All the family are in the crowd, wife, mum and dad, nan. Then you get in the changing room and you can't hear anything outside.

'Then your mind gets focused on the game and back to the reality of playing. It was boiling hot as well which was something else you had to deal with. I wasn't anywhere near match fit as I hadn't been properly training for weeks, so I'd try and get an hour or 70 minutes. I'd lie through my teeth about the injury I picked up on that Monday night – my foot was completely broken when I came off there. It happened when I was scoring. As I shot Paul McGrath came across to block it and I kicked the bottom of his boot. Immediately I knew I'd done some damage; my foot swelled up that night. I thought I was out the final as it was so swollen. I refused to have it x-rayed as I knew it was broken and that would be it. So I iced it all week. I wore my boot in bed the night before the game as I knew that if I didn't wear something I wouldn't get one on the next day. Bobby came round and pulled the covers back. "Why you got boots on?" "Oh, they're new and I'm breaking them in," I told him. Then it was the walk up the tunnel and Liverpool are there waiting, and this is real.'

The England coach Don Howe was a genius when laying out tactics and he made sure all players had special assignments. For Gibson it was one he had never done before. 'Don loved his time at Wimbledon. It was a big shock to those coming from outside to Wimbledon; even Coventry was big compared to Wimbledon. Me and Don did have a conversation about it and how different it was to Arsenal, but he loved it. His only responsibility was coaching and when he finished at one o'clock, he was done. Bob did everything else, the press, the scouting, Bob did his share of coaching, but he was wise enough to let the best coach in the country have the job of managing us lot. Don loved the spirit. Him and Bob wanted to cut down on the yellow and red cards, but he loved our attitude.

'He'd nail all the players. No one was out of reach which can be the case with some managers. If you deserved it, you got it, but his tactical plan for me was to man-mark Alan Hansen which was probably the reason why I thought I could get through the foot and hernia injuries. I could take painkilling pills. I wouldn't get too much of the ball, in fact I've watched the game back and I don't receive a single pass in the whole game. I chased things and try to get knock-downs, but I watched and thought no one has actually passed me the ball. After watching them take apart Forest we then thought, "Oh shit, we could get humiliated." That's when the plans started, but they told us that Forest are the complete opposite of us, they're a nice team, which plays nice football, and barely make a tackle apart from Stuart Pearce, so don't think to judge Liverpool on that game. If Hansen can't bring the ball out, [Steve] McMahon can't get the ball from him, and if he does Vinnie will nail him, and Wise will have Barnes, Thorn and Young play out their game to stop Aldridge, and Fash on Gillespie, Cork on Nicol.'

The goal itself was straight from the training ground, and one that had been seen before, so it was no surprise that the routine paid off. 'It was the same goal as we had scored against Newcastle. Corky was meant to be there, and Sanch was shouting at him to go there, but he didn't so Sanch got there. That was the planning but went slightly different as Corky forgot. He still says, "It should have been me." I was on the penalty spot for anything that got knocked down. Another part of the plan was if Grobbelaar had to kick long it was our aim, as they wouldn't beat Thorn and Young in the air, so we could have that all day long. We needed players to have the game of their life, and those two at the back were phenomenal, they were out of this world. Beasant made some great saves, one from close range, and the penalty, but the two centre-backs were immense.'

Then came the Goodyear penalty incident, and a sense of dread. 'Initially you feel the injustice. You don't get the rub of the green when you play for a small club. That happens, or at least feels like it and I didn't think it was a penalty. I was on the halfway line, but I pretty much went along with the rest of the team. I can see why he gave it, had it been us he might not have, that's harsh to say. I felt aggrieved at the injustice and as Aldridge was so good at penalties I thought "shit, that's it". We'd been hanging on, then Beasant saved it! I came off, and it was awful sitting there. Scales came on and did the same job I'd been doing. He comes on and everyone shouting at him, "Where the fuck you playing?" and he puts his arm out and points up front. "I'm going to run, just run around." He's a great athlete so he was ideal to do that, so the plan didn't change. When the whistle went it was similar to the semi-final, a relief at first. You're counting down the minutes, and the seconds, its going on forever, and when it finished it was like, "Thank god, we hung on, we've won," and you don't know how to celebrate as you've not done it before.'

The boyhood dream had come true. After seeing Spurs win the FA Cup two years in a row, and then Coventry win it a year before, Gibson had followed his dream and won the competition himself. 'I've got a Liverpool scarf that was thrown my way, and I can remember it being emptier not empty,' he said of the celebrations straight after on the pitch. 'There was a lap of honour to be done around a pretty full stadium. It was bewildering, you take the team picture, you're hugging each other, and everyone involved. Then in the changing room after the game it was silent, everyone was quiet, we'd worked so hard, and it was so hot. Don had ice-cold wet towels at half-time, something he picked up with England in Mexico or Spain. Nobody had water, it was tea. Gouldy, my team-mates, Liverpool, and the referee all had white lips as we were all dehydrated! It was just tea and sugar, a few energy drinks but they made you piss as well. We had chicken and beans at lunch, but no water. Dalglish had his ski jacket on as it was a superstition! So tired and drained and quiet, then it got lively after the champagne, but a group of players that had given their all were overwhelmed. We all had a different path to get there.'

Getting back to Plough Lane for the planned celebration could have got out of hand, but calm heads prevailed. 'Vinnie tried to throw Jimmy Hill out, and everyone had the hump as Lulu was there, we didn't want hangers-on. Everyone hated us, if you were Wimbledon great, but we didn't want those jumping on the bandwagon. Vinnie had a row with Gouldy saying, "Get him out, he's slagged us off all year, now he wants to be here." Hill was mates with Bob through his days at Coventry, but it was funny and it didn't turn nasty.

'That night was quite subdued as we were all tired and a couple went off and did their own thing. I think a few players wanted to be on breakfast television at 7am, so they went to bed early. A few of us wanted to go back to the hotel with our wives but we couldn't get a taxi.

'Jason Cundy lived in Wimbledon and he has told me he had one of his greatest nights out when we won, down in the Village, and we were in the marquee, we should have gone to the Village! So, we started walking back, and a police van pulled up so we all jumped in the back and they gave us a lift back to the hotel, and when we got back they'd shut the bar. It was because we misbehaved on the Friday night at dinner, and they didn't want a dozen or so of us sitting until the early hours celebrating. The police should have taken us to the Village.'

The next morning, tired and slightly hungover for those who did get drinks, there was a parade to attend. 'The bus is going 30mph flying through, there's no one about. It was like the Friday night at the pub no one recognised us, even though we've been at Wembley. This could be embarrassing but when we turned the corner, and it was the best surprise, as we genuinely didn't think anyone would be there. That's what winning the cup is all about. It was joyful. An hour later I'm stuck in traffic trying to get back home and I'm thinking, "Did that just happen?" The whole weekend was so surreal, like living a dream, then bang, back to reality stuck in traffic. Corky's testimonial on the Monday was fun, and then I had surgery on the Tuesday. The club changed after that; it wasn't the same. Players wanted to leave. We were the lowest paid in the country, and there was the realisation from other teams that our players could play, so after winning it was never the same, but it was so worth it.'

Seven

Fulfilling the Dream

LUTON TOWN had lost the Simod Cup Final 4-1 to Reading at Wembley Stadium on 27 March. The stadium was becoming a second home for them in the latter part of the season and they would take the experience of playing in front of over 61,000, a healthy crowd for two smaller sides in the Full Members' Cup (Simod being the sponsor at that time). The tournament was devised when English clubs were banned from playing in Europe, although Arsenal, Tottenham, Liverpool and Manchester United had opted out of competing in it. Luton had also reached the League Cup Final, to be played on 24 April against Arsenal, and were taking part in the Mercantile Credit Centenary Festival tournament, which was to be played a week after the FA Cup semi, so a quadruple Wembley visit was on the cards if they could just get one bigger win under their belts.

Wimbledon had never beaten Luton until a month prior to the semi-final, so that mental hurdle had been removed which meant there was nothing to fear, except the fear of playing the biggest game in the club's history. The Dons went into the semi-final as underdogs, not by much, but the experience of Luton in recent big matches had given them the edge at the bookmakers. That didn't matter to Bobby Gould's team as they thrived on it, but it didn't mean they lost respect for their opponents, and captain Dave Beasant was right to point this out, 'I don't think that game [Wimbledon's 2-0 First Division victory on 5 March] was a good guide for judging Luton because the previous week they had reached the Littlewoods Cup Final by beating Oxford and they were just a few days away from the Simod Cup semi-final when they had another chance of reaching Wembley. Their minds might have been on Wembley that day and everyone in the team knows that we could have had a much tougher game against them. We expect a different attitude on Saturday.'

Knowing how far they had come through the season and how they knocked on the door to this round the year before, Beasant knew he was ready for this moment, 'We were guilty of underestimating Tottenham in the quarter-finals and we nearly made the same mistake against Watford this season. We woke up just in time to put things right in that one. It's a relief for me personally. When we lost to Tottenham last season, I wondered if I'd blown my best chance of playing in a cup final. Don Howe told us when he came to the club that a top pro will only get ten chances of getting to

Wembley, one chance per season. I've been playing for nine seasons now, so I think it's time I made my move.'

Wearing the captain's armband for the opposition was someone more well known for another part of strapping. Steve Foster had to wear his famous white headband to protect scar tissue on his forehead, in a similar way that Eric Young would wear his black one. It was now part of his matchday attire and would give him that larger-than-life look when marshalling his defence. The self-confessed 'lousy' striker had been converted into a strong leader at the heart of defence, but it was a slice of fortune that led to his switch. After being rejected by Southampton, Foster was picked up by south coast rivals Portsmouth, managed at that time by Ian St John, and during an injury crisis he was tested at centre-back in a reserve game, to put his height to good use. 'From that point my career changed dramatically. The boss asked me to have a go in that position for the first team and I was happy to help out,' Foster said. A move to Brighton & Hove Albion followed where he made his name, but he missed the FA Cup Final in 1983 due to suspension. The 2-2 draw with Manchester United in the first match – which Albion could have won in the last minute – meant a replay and he would be available, although Brighton got thumped 4-0 in the rematch. Now, five years on he was taking Luton to finals and multiple Wembley trips.

His manager, Ray Harford, had assembled a tidy squad, but with a view to youth as well. He could see the value of bringing the next generation through, 'My first team to some extent takes care of itself. My role there is to organise them and discipline them. The bit I love best is working with the players, particularly the next batch.'

Harford did have one player who was Luton's own version of John Fashanu. After being sent off in the first five minutes on the first day of the season, and then again on Boxing Day, Mick Harford – no relation to his manager – was gaining a reputation as the Hatters' hardman, 'It's more a case of the odd moment of madness rather than being tough, but I know I have got to curb it. Being sent off only harms your team and sitting out the two-match bans is agony. I have always been happy at Luton. We are a happy club and that is important.' Harford was pleased, like Beasant, when it was announced that the semi-final was to be played at White Hart Lane, 'I don't know why, but I always seem to play well there.' Wimbledon were hoping that come 5pm on Saturday, 9 April, Harford would not have had a good day, and some of the happiness had been taken away from his club.

Being on the big stage would not alter Wimbledon's approach. Bobby Gould was too wise and knew that any tampering now would do more harm than good, so it was best to keep with the tried-and-tested way. Despite the injuries the Dons were able to field a near full-strength team with Scales the only one who hadn't played regularly through the campaign so far, but he was more than capable even if early on in his Dons career it didn't seem that way. His worst critic was a team-mate and that's never good news. Fashanu was very much a sink or swim kind of guy when it came to new players finding their way in the ranks, and he could see that the young defender was struggling in training, which he felt was a potential threat to his ability on matchdays. Gould recalled that Fash would openly tell Scales that he couldn't cross, tackle, or be of any basic use. Slowly though he gained the trust and respect which meant he could come into the side and play with confidence. 'A year ago, I wouldn't have dreamed that I would be in this situation,' the blond defender stated.

On the opposite side of the defensive line, Terry Phelan had similar problems adjusting to life in the Crazy Gang. Breaking down in the manager's office, the speedy full-back was helped along by an idea that Gould and Howe had. If you take somebody's strengths and promote them, it will make others realise what potential is there. Knowing that Phelan had pace to burn, they concocted some drills in training that were all about running, sprints, aware that their player would be at the front. From that moment his confidence grew, and the squad accepted Phelan into the fold.

Another main player in the back line was Andy Thorn, who was searching for full England honours after playing several times for the under-21s. He also wanted to rewrite the history lessons that got handed out at the club when the FA Cup came around each year, 'Even now they still show videos of that famous Leeds game down at the club. It would be nice to think that in future years it's us they'll be reminiscing about. If we can go all the way to Wembley, I'm sure they won't forget us. We beat Luton in the league game at Plough Lane the other week, and although it was hardly a classic match, it was very encouraging the way we restricted their number of shooting opportunities to a minimum.'

Football is a game for everyone. It is easy to start playing, and no matter your status it can be enjoyed by all, whether that's participating at any level or watching on television. It is also about opinions, and sometimes those who have theirs broadcast through varying platforms will be heard louder than others. There were plenty in the media and written press who did not like Wimbledon. How they played was simply wrong, a stain on the game, bad for football, and so to reach an FA Cup Final, the showpiece of the domestic calendar and a worldwide event, was just unthinkable. It was often said that if Liverpool, as an example, were to play a ball long and it was flicked, for a striker to volley in, it would be masterful, but when Wimbledon did so it was long-ball tactics that belonged in the dark ages. So what if noses were put out of joint with this style; there was no rule, written or otherwise that said it shouldn't happen.

The two semi-finals would offer a choice for journalists of either neat and tidy, possession-based football or that of grit, heart, and determination of wills. For a long time Wimbledon had played to the strength of their ability, and it carried them all the way to Wembley. The purists didn't know where to look, or what to say. Neither did the over-eager Tottenham steward as a minibus rolled up at the gates. 'You can't come in here,' he said. The driver rolled down the window. 'Oh, yes, we can. We're playing a semi-final today,' he said, as he steered his way in. Bobby Gould was setting the tone for the afternoon.

Just under 26,000 went to north London, a reminder of the size of the two clubs' fanbases, and the attraction of the two for any neutrals. The referee was Keith Hackett and like any official on big matchdays he had done his homework and was also looking not to have any influence on the outcome of the tie. First, however, came breakfast, 'I was delighted to have been appointed to the FA Cup semi-final Wimbledon v Luton Town which took place at White Hart Lane, the home of Tottenham Hotspur. For a number of years I had been sales and marketing director for a company based at Gallows Corner, Romford, and the journey down the M1 and around the North Circular was familiar territory. I travelled to London on the morning of the match, stopping on my way to grab a light meal at a Little Chef. This was a regular habit of mine, usually having eggs on toast and a coffee before every game.'

It was hard for Hackett not to notice that the ground was not full, 'The attendance of around 25,000 was disappointing but the numbers shortfall was made up by the noise of both sets of spectators. I had officiated both teams and was familiar with the players and was fully aware that Jones, Fashanu, Wise and Sanchez could be a handful. In the build-up to kick-off, you could not fail to hear the very loud music coming out of Wimbledon's dressing room. They came out into the tunnel laughing and joking, showing no sign of nerves. I remained alert and fortunately, the players of both teams were on their best behaviour. Vinnie Jones was always regarded as the one player to keep an eye on, but my focus was on Lawrie Sanchez who would stir things up with the occasional off-the-ball challenge. John Fashanu was the most articulate player that I had officiated, and I knew that I had to keep an eye on his flailing arms.'

Don Howe was prepared also, and after studying the Simod Cup Final tapes his message to the players was to exploit a weak offside trap just as Reading had done in beating the Hatters. The over-the-top balls would work, but Wimbledon had to be more than one-dimensional, utilising quick through balls, and turning the defence around on the ground as well as in the air. They had to be smart.

Luton had Andy Dibble in goal, standing in for the injured Les Sealey, and at first it looked like it could be a very long afternoon for the young Welshman. In the very first minute he got caught in no-man's land trying to collect a throw but was bumped by Gibson before Wise could head into an empty goal. It was an early let-off but within moments he was punching air as he mistimed a cross and was lucky that Ashley Grimes was covering behind to clear. Dibble grew into the game after this nervous start, even if his protective line ahead of him didn't, and on a few occasions he had to bail them out. Cork and Wise were pulling the strings, and with neat exchanges to the front pair of Fashanu and Terry Gibson they were looking dangerous, but each time Dibble was on hand to snuff out the attacks. One save he would have been most pleased with came when Fashanu broke clear of the high offside trap and tore through on goal, with Gibson and Sanchez in support to his left. The ball took an awful bobble on a muddy centre strip of the pitch, which was enough to just take it out of control from Fashanu's stride and give enough time for Dibble to smother at his feet. Foster was unusually careless with a back-pass and Dibble again was on hand to push Fashanu wider than he liked and another good chance vanished. Then it was Sanchez who was sloppy, letting a loose pass go which Danny Wilson locked on to, only for Beasant to be equally quick with a tidy save, and half-time arrived with neither goal breached.

'Don't start feeling sorry for yourselves if you don't win the game because you've had enough chances already to be on the way to Wembley!' was the offering that Gould made at the interval, and it was true. Wimbledon had sprung the offside trap a handful of times but had nothing to show for it.

Luton were more assertive when the game got back under way. Wilson was lively and got the ball from Tim Breacker on the right flank, before his cross was helped on by Mark Stein over the head of Young, and then from inside the box Mick Harford rifled home a hip-height volley. It was a good goal, one that was suited to the game as both teams were trying to avoid a constant aerial bombardment which would have been an easy pattern to fall into, but this attack only had the ball on the ground once as it bounced up for Harford. Luton were now in the ascendency and had two quick corners, the second of which was cleared only as far as the edge of the box where Wilson met the ball with a clean volley that Beasant saved comfortably.

Wimbledon got themselves level ten minutes after going behind, and it was the first true error that Dibble had made. Going to gather a corner from Wise he was outside the six-yard box with Fashanu and Foster also competing for the cross. Put off his run, Dibble dropped the ball, and as Gibson collected, the goalkeeper tried to make amends but only succeeded in bringing down the striker. Gibson jumped up with both fists clenched and let out a scream of delight, and then Jones grabbed him and planted a big kiss on his head. The 21st goal of Fashanu's great season was a side-footed penalty that belied the tension of the occasion. Cork remembered it for other reasons, 'I don't think anyone has ever kicked the ball slower. Dibble almost had time to get up after diving the wrong way and walk over and stop it!' There was instant relief and euphoria on the pitch and in the stands and terraces. The tables had turned and Wimbledon had the belief. Wise was starting to get on the ball more in areas that could affect the game and when he twisted away from his marker on the left his deep cross was headed back across goal, but Fashanu's aim was off with a header from six yards out.

With ten minutes remaining, Cork was wide on the right and sent over a blind cross for anyone willing and gambling in the box. The striker looked back, 'We'd just got a throw-in and it came to me. We'd been practising hooking the ball in, and here was my chance to do exactly that. I just slung the ball in the middle.' Wise was the most alert and stretched with everything he had, so much so that he needed both legs to get a full and proper connection on the ball. Had it been a player he touched first it would have been an instant dismissal and fate would have taken another strange twist. Thankfully he got the ball, and it dribbled underneath Dibble for a 2-1 lead. Wise immediately leaped up and sprinted to the halfway line and the Dons dugout, arm high in the air, grin as wide as the Wandle River is long. 'The emotion of the moment got the better of me then,' the winning goalscorer said. 'I just got up and kept running, and running, and running. I wasn't running anywhere in particular. All the lads were trying to catch me. The first person I saw was Terry Gibson. I just jumped on him, and the rest of the lads piled on top.'

Gibson, who had recently left the field having worked hard all afternoon, was indeed the first to greet Wise and they jumped into each other's awkward embrace. Gibson recalled, 'I hadn't played or trained for a few weeks because of my knee injury so I was very tired, but the exhaustion was worth it. I started to get cramp and Bobby Gould knew I was struggling. You can't con him, so I came off. I wanted to run on [to celebrate] but the linesman was nearby so I thought I'd better not but then Wise charged towards me and so I thought "what the heck" and joined in the celebration.' It didn't take long before the rest of the team were also jumping on the pair, with Gould trying to keep everything calm, which was nigh-on impossible in these heady moments. Don Howe leant out the dugout and put both hands out wide, signifying the amount of time left. It was agonisingly close. 'I've got the knack of nicking the important goals,' Wise said. 'I got the one that put us on top of the table last season but the one against Luton was far more important.'

When the final whistle blew the roar would have been heard back at Plough Lane. The bench cleared with smiles and hugs. 'At the final whistle, it just seemed that we had won another game but gradually as the day went on it started to sink in. There's no end to things that can happen to the club now,' Beasant said happily. The party didn't stop on the terraces and in the dressing room, as everyone went back to Nelsons nightclub at Plough Lane. 'It was nonstop drinking. No one went home. We played together, we battled together, and we drank together,' said Cork, who was going to let this moment last as long as possible. 'I was in tears, but Don Howe was being very casual about it all. It was something like his seventh cup final, but for me, it was very, very special.'

Gould was still trying his best to keep a lid on his emotions, 'We will continue to play the power football that has given this wonderful club such success. Teams don't like playing against it and we are going to continue stuffing it down their throats. Even international players panic when you launch high balls at them. If Dave Beasant can catch hold of a few clearances and get the ball into the opposite box, we'll see what happens. We're the underdogs again [in the final], what have we got to lose?' He was serious when talking to the press afterwards, 'If we can put on a little bit in the last third, we shall be a very, very good club. We haven't got to be so direct at times.'

It was hard to digest what had just happened for those who had doubted, but such was the attitude at the club, and of Gould, that thoughts were already looking beyond the rest of the 1987/88 season, even with a Wembley final now on the fixture list. With the ban on English clubs competing in Europe up for discussion at a UEFA meeting in June, Wimbledon would be the country's representative in the Cup Winners' Cup given that even if the ban were lifted Liverpool would have an extension. Bobby Gould said,

'If Mr Moynihan [Colin, the Conservative government's sports minister] behaves himself and Mrs Thatcher goes along with her famous words that if Wimbledon can reach the First Division then anybody can achieve anything and make sure that English clubs get back, who knows what might happen at Plough Lane next season.'

Eleven years earlier Wimbledon were still in the Southern League; five years previously they were in the Fourth Division and now they could be facing Barcelona in the Nou Camp. An FA spokesman confirmed, 'If Liverpool do not win the championship, but do win the FA Cup, we would have to ask UEFA's permission to enter Wimbledon because of Liverpool's extended ban, although that is unlikely to be necessary. If we are invited back in, the maximum number of clubs we would be allowed to represent us would be four, one in both the European Cup and Cup Winners' Cup and two in the UEFA Cup. Liverpool would not be allowed in the European Cup, and neither would the runners-up thus reducing it to three. But Wimbledon as runners-up in the FA Cup would be able to participate in the competition. Wimbledon's ground is up to the standards required for First Division football and so they should meet the necessary requirements set out by UEFA.'

This was music to Sam Hammam's ears, the Dons' owner and managing director. 'We are proud of our humble origins,' he stated, after saying that European football would be played in the club's non-league-style ground, should they be allowed to enter. 'We do not have any complexes about Plough Lane. If Barcelona or Real Madrid go into our dressing rooms, they will have a complex.'

There was still a page to be written in this script, though.

What a difference a week makes. With all the excitement around the club you'd have been forgiven if you forgot there was a league season to finish, as there were now two Wembley trips to look forward to, one no sooner than the week immediately after seeing Luton off. One player though would be missing the first trip, as Andy Thorn returned from England under-21 duty with a groin injury; it was a double blow as the Three Lions lost 4-2 to France in the first leg of the European Championship semi-final.

His place was taken by Peter Cawley. Making your debut at Wembley would be something you'd hope to look back on with great fondness, but in the shortened matches of 20 minutes each way it was over before Cawley and the rest knew it. For the Mercantile Credit tournament, the only other change from the victorious team of seven days before was that of Brian Gayle for Vinnie Jones. It was a surreal moment seeing the Dons walk out at Wembley with pockets of fans from each of the 16 teams dotted around the big stadium, with the neutral supporters sitting where they could, a far cry from the blue and red sea that was in store a month later. Being the first game, and on a wet morning, a ten o'clock start clearly wasn't suited to the Dons as Fourth Division Tranmere Rovers beat them 1-0. The goal was in the 27th minute, David Martindale going clean through and beating Beasant with a well-placed shot. Gibson had Wimbledon's best chance but smashed his effort far too high. Rovers would go on to beat Newcastle (who had beaten Liverpool) to reach the Sunday semi-final, which they lost on penalties to eventual winners Nottingham Forest. Small consolation for missing the real Wembley final.

Back in the league, relegation-threatened Portsmouth visited Plough Lane for a match that will be remembered not for Wise opening and closing the scoring but for Pompey goalkeeper Alan Knight being helped off the field in just the second minute and the ugly confrontations that followed. It looked like John Fashanu was getting the blame after an elbow caught Knight hard and left him with a suspected broken cheekbone. A melee followed with Micky Quinn and Noel Blake squaring up and starting a shoving contest with the striker. Referee Allan Gunn took a while to bring the boiling pot down to simmering, and Lee Sandford was withdrawn from his left-back position to put on the gloves and hold the FA Cup finalists at bay. He did so for all of 15 minutes, only being beaten when Wise's drive from just outside the box took a vicious deflection to leave him stranded.

The rain-affected pitch was keeping nice football at a premium, but Pompey boss Alan Ball kept faith, and after an hour got his reward. Kevin Dillon, who had been a delayed substitute during the earlier switching of goalkeepers, and gave away the free kick that led to the Dons' goal, made amends by floating over an inviting set piece of his own for veteran striker Paul Mariner to place a header past Beasant. Fifteen minutes on Dillon became goalscorer and hero as he applied a neat finish to Billy Gilbert's through ball.

Desperate for the points, Ball knew that Pompey had to dig in, but Wise produced a great response and scored just a few minutes from the end to prevent a crucial three points going back down the A3. 'You have to fight for the right to play your football here, or you get walked on,' Ball reported afterwards, and he also had to issue an apology to Fashanu on behalf of his players. 'The lads all say it was Eric Young,' he said, referring to Knight's now stitched-up face, and fractured jaw.

The visit of Chelsea always brought a few extra fans through the gate, so that and the chance to see the Dons in their last Saturday home match before their big day out meant that the 23 April encounter attracted the largest attendance of the season at Plough Lane. It was unusual to have so many star players out, but when the roll call of the two teams happened it was disappointing that Fashanu, Gibson and Cork were missing, adding to the absence of the suspended Jones. Jones had his deputy in Vaughan Ryan, John Gannon replaced Gibson, Paul Miller came in for Cork, and a debut was given to Dave Swindlehurst, who had joined the club on non-contract terms but seemed a yard off the pace. Sanchez and Wise were running the midfield and early on Chelsea didn't have an answer to the less physical line-up that faced them. Sanchez got the first goal, and afterwards sent out a message, 'People get the idea we're a one-man team. I think we've shown today how untrue that is. If fans follow all the media coverage, it's easy to get the impression this club is made by one person alone. But I think the rest of us demonstrated today how unfair that is by producing some of the best football this club has played. In fact we were enjoying it so much that we began giggling among ourselves in the first half because it was all going so easily.'

It wasn't a complete performance as Wise missed a penalty, one he had argued with and fought Terry Phelan for. He did get his goal though and the match looked out of reach halfway through the second 45 minutes. Eric Young offered a lifeline to the Blues with a rash challenge in the box and Gordon Durie knocked in the penalty, and the Scot grabbed a second with a little under ten minutes to play, when Beasant lost a high ball in the sun, to give Chelsea an unexpected and undeserved point in their relegation scrap. 'At the end we were just sitting in the dressing room dazed because after being brilliant for 80 minutes we gave two goals away. Chelsea must be laughing their heads off. With that kind of good fortune, they will definitely escape relegation,' said Sanchez, no longer in high spirits.

Roy Law collects the FA Amateur Cup in 1963

Dickie Guy held aloft after the 0-0 draw
at Leeds United

Dave Bassett masterminded the
Dons' rise up the leagues

Laurie Cunningham made his debut in the Newcastle FA Cup match, and tries to get the ball off Mirandinha

Bobby Gould tries to calm the team down after the semi-final winner

Dennis Wise, Alan Cork and Andy Thorn recording the Cup Final song at Abbey Road

Liverpool fans' humour before the Cup Final

The players get their first taste of the Cup Final atmosphere on their pre-match walkabout

Lawrie Sanchez watches as his flicked header wins the FA Cup

Dave Beasant saves John Aldridge's penalty, the first one saved in an FA Cup Final

Relief at the final whistle

Dave Beasant lifts the cup with the team behind him

Terry Phelan celebrates the win with Don Howe and Bobby Gould

Bobby Gould shows his joy after the game

Clive Goodyear celebrating with Dave Beasant and Lawrie Sanchez

The town centre welcomes home the team

The team on the Town Hall steps

One player who was not showing any signs of good humour was 19-year-old Vaughan Ryan, who would miss the FA Cup Final. Able to slot into the Vinnie Jones role in the side, he left Plough Lane with a broken cheek and jaw after a clash with Steve Wicks. It didn't look a fair challenge and Gould was incensed, but Chelsea caretaker boss Bobby Campbell was quick to defend his man, suggesting Wicks was 'not in the least to blame'. Wicks himself, who would later visit Ryan in hospital as he was in recovery, explained how he saw it, 'The ball was there to be won and I hit him after I won it. I struck him with my shoulder, not my elbow. I'm not dirty.' Ryan had already fought back from a similar injury in November after breaking his jaw in three places against Southampton, but this setback ended his season and the dream of playing in the biggest game of his fledgling career.

In the programme notes for Wimbledon's trip to Nottingham Forest, Brian Clough was quick to heap praise on the Dons, 'I'm only sorry this is our last meeting with Wimbledon this season. It would have been nice to have met them again on 14 May but that wasn't to be. Don't let anyone say they don't deserve to be there. When they turn up at Wembley, I hope they enjoy every single minute of it. I'm delighted for Bobby Gould and Don Howe that they have done it, not only with one of the unfashionable clubs in the First Division, but one of the most unfashionable in the Football League. I know we'll have our hands full this afternoon despite the fact that Wimbledon are looking forward to Wembley. Other teams might let FA Cup thoughts creep in at this stage of the season, but I doubt whether it has even entered their heads.' What followed was a 0-0 draw, although there have been worse goalless games. Swindlehurst was again deputising for Fashanu but was replaced by Robbie Turner. The sub couldn't get past Steve Sutton when one-on-one, then in the late stages Andy Thorn handled a cross from Andy Rice, but Beasant saved Rice's spot kick.

The congested schedule due to the cup runs and weather-forced cancellations meant that Wimbledon's final three league games would be played in six days, leaving just five days before the final. Sheffield Wednesday were the final visitors to Plough Lane of the season, the home fans' last chance to see their team until they would emerge from that long tunnel at Wembley. It was another large crowd for a midweek fixture, largely due to the voucher scheme that had been devised to guarantee a ticket for the final. Supporters paying on the gate at the final three home matches collected a voucher. All three could then be exchanged, with the appropriate cash value, for a cup final ticket. It was open to a bit of abuse but given the large allocation to fans of both competing teams, it was very unlikely that Wimbledon would sell all of theirs, and those who wanted to go would find a way of getting a ticket. This scheme though was favourable and if nothing else it swelled the attendance for those games, and also the anticipation as fans clutched their different-numbered and coloured vouchers tightly. It was a virtual full-strength side that played out a 1-1 draw, with Laurie Cunningham at number 11 instead of Wise, and remarkably Clive Goodyear was back, recovered from his broken leg and in ahead of John Scales. Terry Gibson, also returning to the side, took just three minutes to put the Dons ahead, proving his value again, but Lee Chapman scored an equaliser in the second half to share the points.

The last Saturday of the season had the Dons on their travels to Norwich City and the only changes were to rotate Cunningham and Wise, and Brian Gayle for Eric Young. This was clearly a case of keeping players healthy, and with both teams having nothing to play for in terms of altering their league positions it was an ordinary game. It was decided late on when Gibson ran on to a poor back-pass by Tony Spearing in the 82nd minute to give Wimbledon their first league win in nine games.

The season concluded with what is usually one of the most anticipated fixtures on the list, a trip to Old Trafford, but on a Monday night when preparations for the FA Cup Final should have been under way, it was just a case of going through the motions and trying to keep healthy, as well as gaining some possible momentum. Terry Gibson was on fire to finish the season and got his third goal in as many appearances; this one was extra special as it was against his old team where he had a torrid time. The Dons were good value for their half-time lead but United were on a really good run at the end of a long campaign and took over after the interval, Brian McClair scoring twice to take his season total to 32, the winner a penalty given away by Terry Phelan for handball.

Behind the scenes the phones in the club offices were constantly ringing with queries about tickets for the final and their availability. A structure was put in place that was deemed the fairest for loyal supporters, especially those who were in possession of season tickets. Those who held them had a specific date of 26 April to submit their applications for tickets, which was also the case for club members. Tickets were priced at £30, £25, £17.50 and £10 depending on the location in the stadium, with terrace tickets a very reasonable £8. Regardless of where your season ticket was at Plough Lane you could apply for four tickets. As a reward for being a club member but not a season ticket holder you could apply for two tickets.

To push loyalty for those who weren't fortunate enough to have either a season ticket or membership, you could cash in the vouchers collected at the last three home games for a guaranteed ticket for the final. This would also apply if you had a seat ticket for that trio of games as well. The morning after the final home match against Sheffield Wednesday, a queue started to form outside the club offices well before the advertised opening time of 10am, even though the tickets would be available through normal working hours. Details also emerged of a possible replay date and time. Should the Dons be able to hold league champions Liverpool to a draw the replay would be at the same venue, on the Thursday of the following week, again with priority going to season ticket holders and members on the Sunday after the first game, with all other tickets going on general sale the day after. Another day for the fans to put in their diaries was that of 20 August, when the traditional curtain-raiser to the new season, the Charity Shield, would be played. These were certainly times that the club had not seen before, and extra volunteers were drafted in to help with the administration side of things.

Wimbledon Football Club were going to Wembley Stadium for an FA Cup Final against the best club side in all of Europe.

Eight

Preparation

We Are Wimbledon – The 1988 Wimbledon FA Cup Final Squad

Though the road we walk is long, so far and wide,
We know that you are always on our side.
Jump for joy when we score,
Hear it loud – the Super Dons roar.
Play for Wimbledon: who could ask for more?

Swaying side by side, together, here we go,
Go for Wimbledon, forever, ever more.
We'll give it all that we've got,
Keep on reaching for the top,
And you know we'll never let you down.
So come on, join the south-west London sound.

We are Wimbledon. Up and at 'em, here we go!
Singing Wimbledon, wave the colours to and fro.

Go with Wimbledon, follow us and see us through,
Shout and sing for the boys who fear no one,
Proud to wear the blue of Wimbledon.

So all together, see us on our way,
Playing hard and fair the game we love to play.
We reign supreme in our Plough Lane home,
Where we never walk alone,
And you know we'll never let you down.
So come on join the south-west London sound.

We are Wimbledon. Up and at 'em, here we go!
Singing Wimbledon, wave the colours to and fro.
Go with Wimbledon, follow us and see us through,
Shout and sing for the boys who fear no one,
Proud to wear the blue of Wimbledon.

We are Wimbledon. Up and at 'em, here we go!
Singing Wimbledon, wave the colours to and fro.
Go with Wimbledon, follow us and see us through,
Shout and sing for the boys who fear no one,
Proud to wear the blue of Wimbledon.

As part of the build-up to the final the club created a souvenir brochure. There would be other unofficial magazines to whet the appetite as the big day got closer, but the club with its close connections to its fans designed a neat and tidy A4-sized, yellow-and-blue-paged insight as to how Wimbledon had reached Wembley with notes on those who had led the way. It was fitting that, in the style of that season's programmes, manager Bobby Gould would have the first words. His thoughts were honest and genuine as he stated, 'If somebody had told me when I joined the club in June last year, that for the 1987/88 season, I would be leading the Wimbledon team out on to the hallowed turf of Wembley for the FA Cup Final, I might have thought they were talking gobbledygook!'

He wasn't wrong. Even though the Dons had seen a glimpse of what it could be like in the season before, it would be a brave person to think they could achieve every player's and fan's dream of going that extra couple of steps that they couldn't take in 1987.

Gould continued, 'As Wimbledon manager, I hope we long continue to surprise the rest of the football world.' He went on to recall moments of his own playing career, having got to Wembley twice, and knowing the importance of getting to a Wembley final for players, with how much they sacrifice, 'I am sure that when the parents of the players started following their sons on their footballing careers from the parks in and around Wimbledon, Derby, London and wherever, they never envisaged in their wildest dreams seeing their son walk out on to Wembley and to be there to share their occasion. I only hope that win, lose or draw, people can walk away from the "Mecca" of world football and say, "That was a day to remember."'

Trying to draw on some inspiration for his beloved team who had been successful in 1987, Gould continued, 'I am Coventry born and bred. I watched them in the Third Division South and Fourth Division days so their win at Wembley was a great moment. I was especially pleased with the seven or eight players I had taken to the club.' With that shock victory over Spurs, Coventry had set a blueprint of how to beat more favoured opponents, and with the experience that some Wimbledon players had with recent cup runs Gould was confident that another upset could be completed, 'The spirit at this club is something very special and, on their day, they can beat anyone. The best buy in British football this season has definitely been a Wimbledon season ticket because every holder has been able to buy four top-quality Wembley tickets. That's even better than Peter Beardsley! We only have 6,000 loyal supporters, yet we still don't seem to have enough tickets to go round. Heaven knows how Liverpool manage.'

Where the manager had his past couple of Wembley experiences to fall back on, his coach Don Howe had even more. He had been able to savour the atmosphere no fewer than six times as a player, but now his job was to keep the Wimbledon squad grounded while also devising a plan that would undo their more illustrious opponents. 'In a way, there's something extra special because the Arsenal were expected to do it,' Howe said of his four FA Cup trips and two League Cup visits with the Gunners. 'For

Wimbledon, it is a terrific achievement, and it is naturally very exciting.'

The artisan in Howe didn't know what to expect after he took his old team-mate's offer up and joined him at Plough Lane and the open expanse of training area off the A3, 'I had read a lot of stuff about them in the press but I have since found out that 90 per cent of that coverage was rubbish. I went to Sweden on the club's pre-season tour and I realised what a great set of lads they are. They are good characters and I knew that things would be OK and that the club would at least achieve stability in Division One.'

One thing discussed over the season was the players' discipline. It got out of hand at one stage with frequent suspensions and the club being accused in the media and by the FA of bringing the game into disrepute. It was addressed and the situation vastly improved. Howe didn't want the team to lose their physical edge though as it was part of their DNA, 'The players here use criticism as a stepping stone to go out and compete. That's how it should be.' Then, turning his thoughts to his active role in coaching the team to a historic win, he said, 'If I have to make changes in tactics or give advice I hope I am able to put things right but whatever happens I know the lads won't give up and we will fight all the way to win the cup.'

There were key match-ups all over the pitch that could determine the outcome and where the FA Cup would be headed. The most anticipated among the media was the meeting of Steve McMahon and Vinnie Jones. Both men were known for hard tackling and being their team's lead enforcer on the pitch. Of course, playing for Liverpool, McMahon also drew the plaudits for the way he could pass the ball around, and he had a fierce shot as well. Those who had studied Jones's play would also know that he too could have a handy pass up his sleeve, and with a cracking shot added to his arsenal. One keen observer was the man who Vinnie had very close contact with during the season, Paul Gascoigne. The midfield maestro had come up against both players in the season and had some advice for the Wimbledon man, 'This will be a big test for Vinnie and it will be interesting to see how he handles the occasion. Against a side like Liverpool, especially in the FA Cup Final at Wembley, he'd be wise to concentrate on playing football rather than running around the field mouthing off and doing what he normally does every week. The second time I played against him, in the FA Cup a couple of weeks after our first meeting, he tried to play football and did well. That will be his best bet.'

McMahon himself wouldn't be immediately drawn into the talk of a possible battle with Jones, instead concentrating on his team, 'With this season's side, our opponents have no idea who they're supposed to stop. If they bottle up John Aldridge, Peter Beardsley will score. If they stop both of them, John Barnes is likely to come up with something brilliant. All of the midfield can put the ball away and even Steve Nicol has scored a hat-trick.' Jones, though, was trying to put his bad reputation to bed. His visits to the FA headquarters at Lancaster Gate had been well publicised, 'I had to live with it for months and I'm only just over it. But the new manager and the lads rallied round to help me through and I'm now a stronger person for it. I'm becoming as much a ball player as a ball winner. Don Howe has made me a better player and, while I'm no fancy dan, I see myself more as an old-fashioned right-half. We owe our aggression and will to win to Dave Bassett, but since Bobby Gould and Don Howe arrived, we have developed into a better footballing side.'

John Barnes had just completed the best season of his career, but needed a Wembley win to lock it down as one of the best by any player. He also needed to conquer his Wembley demons, 'My previous two visits at club level both ended in agony. The first by way of cup final defeat in 1984 and more recently, because of an injury I picked up during the centenary festival. I will also be the first to admit that not all my England appearances have been that memorable.'

Playing for Watford against Everton in the final four years earlier had given Barnes a taste of the game at the highest level, but his side just couldn't compete with the blue half of Merseyside as the Toffees were too experienced and on their way to becoming a major force. The injury at the festival forced the winger out for several games, and he missed Liverpool's championship-clinching match against Tottenham. 'I can still claim to have played my part in the title triumph, but it was frustrating to have to sit that one out,' he said. Back to full fitness and hoping to be selected for the European Championship as part of Bobby Robson's 22-man England squad, Barnes knew that Wimbledon would be a tough nut to crack, calling them, 'A tough, hard-working side who will make up for their lack of experience of the big occasion with typical grit and determination.'

Someone who was looking at Barnes like an idol not too far in the past was John Fashanu, but now he was the one looked at and admired, not just by the fans who went to Plough Lane every other week but also by those who rated him as the next £1m man in the transfer market, talk that he played down. Instead, Fashanu wanted to make an impression on the field that would shake off his image of being just a hot-headed physical presence. 'I'm not going to change just because I'm playing in a cup final, and the rest of the lads will be the same. That's the Wimbledon way. Please don't think I'm being flash, but I'm not the type to be affected by nerves. I never have been. We won't freeze this time,' he said, referring to the Tottenham quarter-final loss of 1987. Fashanu's nerve was tested in the semi-final against Luton with a critical penalty that he converted. He admitted, 'Ever since I saw Sócrates take penalties for Brazil in the World Cup I've copied his style. I pick a corner and go for it. I don't believe you have to kick the ball extra hard.'

The Wimbledon players had come from nowhere to form the most formidable team of 'Raggedy-Arse Rovers', as Fashanu had so often called them, that the top flight of English football had seen. Opponents Liverpool were the aristocrats of the game, and were the complete opposite, with big-money signings and fast, one-touch football, managed by one of Europe's top players. It's worth looking at exactly what Wimbledon would be up against in their bid for FA Cup glory.

Kenny Dalglish was the latest Liverpool manager from a long succession to have come through the famous 'bootroom'. Bill Shankly started a philosophy of football that brought huge success through the late 1960s and was furthered when Bob Paisley took over the job in the 70s and they became multiple European Cup winners. Joe Fagan was next in line, and the wins kept coming, but Fagan decided to step away sooner than expected and there was no immediate person on the staff to take over. Keeping it within the club, they looked at their instrumental striker Dalglish, who was still very much an active player, so he agreed to become player-manager. They won the league and cup double in his first season in charge, quite the start. After a season of near misses the 37-year-old, who was still registered as a player at the time of the final, said, 'I cannot treat myself any different from the other players on the staff. Selection depends on how well they are playing.' Dalglish invested in the team though with the likes of

Barnes, Beardsley and Aldridge on board for what was an incredible season. The Scot said, 'There's no secret. The club just employs people who are good at their job, on the field and off it.'

Bruce Grobbelaar, 30, Durban then Zimbabwe. Firmly established as the number one choice in goal after seven years at Anfield. After starting his career with Vancouver Whitecaps, he turned bootroom heads while at Crewe Alexandra and was snapped up for £250,000.

Ronnie Whelan, 26, Dublin. A crowd favourite known for his eye for a cracking goal, Ireland international, and a left-sided midfielder. Made his debut in 1981 and made an instant impact with a goal.

Barry Venison, 23, Consett. Rising up through the youth ranks at Sunderland, he was no stranger to Wembley as he played for his hometown club in the 1985 League Cup Final. An England under-21 player, the full-back signed for the Reds for £150,000.

Gary Ablett, 22, Liverpool. One of the younger players in the squad, who had made progress through Liverpool's youth teams. A couple of loan spells away served him well and he made his debut earlier in the 1987/88 season at full-back.

Ray Houghton, 26, Glasgow. It cost Liverpool £825,000 to secure the midfielder from Oxford United, after he was wanted by several other clubs too. Having started his playing career in London with West Ham

United and Fulham, Houghton became an exciting part of the line-up.

Steve McMahon, 26, Liverpool. After over a century of appearances for neighbours Everton he made a switch to Aston Villa in 1983. The 1987/88 season was his third on the other side of Stanley Park, having cost the Reds £350,000. A full England international.

Jan Mølby, 24, Jutland. Enjoyed the double in 1986 and was a key player in the Danish side in the World Cup in the same year. Possessing a thumping shot, he arrived on Merseyside from Dutch side Ajax in 1984.

Peter Beardsley, 27, Newcastle. One of the most sought-after players in the country after an excellent World Cup in Mexico, so much so that by 1988 he was Britain's most expensive player at £2m from Newcastle United. Was part of the entertaining Beardsley–Keegan–Waddle attack for the Geordies in 1983.

Alan Hansen, 32, Alloa. A stalwart in the heart of defence with his no-nonsense style. Great passer of the ball, captain of the club. A Scotland international but did not go to the World Cup. He had spent over a decade at Anfield after his switch from Partick Thistle.

Gary Gillespie, 27, Stirling. It could have been very different but choosing Liverpool over Arsenal in 1983 turned out to be the right move for the central defender. Another Scottish international, he settled in alongside his captain in 1987/88.

Nigel Spackman, 27, Romsey. In 1980 he made his debut for Bournemouth, then three years later moved to London when Chelsea saw his talent. After over a year at Liverpool, and having to bide his time to get into the team, he was now a regular choice.

Steve Nicol, 26, Irvine. Another Scottish player who had made himself one of the first on the team sheet. A versatile player who can line up either in defence or midfield, with a nose for a goal as well.

Craig Johnston, 27, Johannesburg. The shaggy perm and Aussie accent were a giveaway when this player was nearby. After his early days in Sydney, he was tempted by the bright lights of Middlesbrough. Then in 1981 Liverpool came knocking with £650,000 to prise him away.

John Barnes, 24, Jamaica. Beardsley may have been the most expensive, but Barnes was the best player. Part of a Watford team that rose through the leagues, he gained full honours for England and played in the 1986 World Cup. Signed for £900,000.

John Aldridge, 29, Liverpool. The top scorer in 1987/88 and no wonder as he scored in the first nine league games of the season, also the team's penalty taker. The Ireland forward was a goal machine, having scored for Newport County, and Oxford United, before his £750,000 transfer.

Liverpool's route to the final did not see them concede a goal until the semi-final stage, but they also had to play one game more than Wimbledon. In the third round,

Stoke City held them to a goalless draw at the Victoria Ground, and did well in the replay to lose by just a single Beardsley goal. In the next round they had another away tie, at Aston Villa, but had little problem with Beardsley on target again, and Barnes getting the other in a 2-0 win. The last 16 gave them a Merseyside derby. Everton were keen to get one over their bitter rivals as they would let their league title slip into their neighbours' hands. Houghton got the only goal at Goodison Park to put the Reds into the quarter-finals, and another away game, this time at Maine Road. This was a much easier tie and Manchester City just couldn't live with a team that was reaching the peak of its powers. Houghton, Beardsley, Johnston and Barnes were all on the scoresheet.

Brian Clough had never won the FA Cup and was perhaps hoping for anyone but the Liverpool goal machine in the last four, but the draw wasn't kind and the top two teams in the competition faced off at Hillsborough. Clough's Nottingham Forest side was one of the finest put together outside of Anfield, and many suggested that this was the real FA Cup Final. Both teams played with purpose and skill but two Aldridge goals sent Liverpool to Wembley. The first came with a little over ten minutes played, from the penalty spot, after Steve Chettle fouled Barnes. Aldridge stepped up and went the same way as he had done a week before against the same opponents in one of the team's best performances in many years. Amazingly, this was Aldridge's first goal of the competition so far that season. Just five minutes after the break he got his second. A fluid move involving the two best players of the season, Beardsley and Barnes, had the latter slide a perfect pass into the Irishman's path. His run was perfectly timed, but he was the first to acknowledge the play of his team-mate, 'It was a great cross, I only had to put my foot on it.' Liverpool were in full flow now and looked likely to add to the score, but Forest kept at their task and were rewarded with a quarter of the game left. A long throw and flick-on caused some panic in the area and Grobbelaar could only push the ball on to Hansen, and as it dropped Nigel Clough was first to it to stab the ball in. Forest could sense a way back, but try as they might no equaliser was forthcoming.

'We had a good crack at it, but the better team won,' Brian Clough said after the match, hiding his disappointment. Still full of praise for his team-mates, Aldridge said, 'It's brilliant playing for this team. There's so much of the ball that it's easy to play. Everything is simple.'

The Captain's Story – Part One
Dave Beasant

IT WAS a long way from the early days at Edgware Town, but after being ever-present for the best part of eight seasons, Dave Beasant was about to play the biggest game of his career so far. No, not the FA Cup Final; it was a dull day at Mansfield Town in the fourth round, but it would change everything. 'That game was quite strange because we got held up in traffic on the way there, and the team sheet had to be handed in 30 minutes before in those days. We were on the bus, and we couldn't get there. We could see the stadium but couldn't get nearer to it because of the traffic, so me and [Bobby] Gould had to jump off and run to the ground to hand the sheet in otherwise we'd have been fined, so we had to leg it through the fans to do that.' The club couldn't afford another fine on top of all the fuss that was being created with their disciplinary record, but this was the glory of the cup at stake.

'The game was on a really muddy pitch, and we were two up, and [Brian] Gayle played a back-pass to me and he under-hit it a bit. I had to come out to clear it, but it was muddy and I've done an air kick. The ball just bounced over my foot, and they scored from that to make it 2-1.' As with any underdog with their tails up the home team came forward with more intent and won themselves a penalty. 'The irony of the penalty was that the night before we were having our evening meal and on the local television, they had a preview about the game and it showed them taking a penalty in a league game, and I though I'll remember that. We didn't have all the footage in those days, so we were lucky as you didn't have team reports and stuff, so I thought he's the penalty taker, so he put it to my left. When they got the penalty, I thought I'll go left, and saved it. When I was interviewed about the save, I told them the story but the fella who took the penalty I'd seen taken, didn't even play! So it could have ended up all so differently, but it was an important save late on.' That strange twist of fate could have ended the run early. Instead, it kick-started Wimbledon's road to glory.

The next round had another away day, and the team that would soon be home to the captain. Beasant said, 'During the game [Andy] Thorn and me were winding Mirandinha up, Thorny more than me. In those days you could back-pass so I'd throw it out to Thorny and he'd wait for Mirandinha to come and shut him down, then roll it back to me and I'd pick it up. That would wind him up through most the game. I remember Thorny wiping his face as Mirandinha had been spitting in his face every time he chased and shut him down. Thorny gave the ball back and he would spit in his face, it was during the whole game. Then, at the end we were all celebrating the win, the ground was being done up so in the Gallowgate End our dressing rooms were in portacabins behind the goal. We're in the centre of the pitch and suddenly I got booted up the backside. I've looked over my left shoulder and this fat bloke was running, so I thought it must have been him, but as I've looked again out the corner of my right eye I could see Terry Gibson sprinting, but he's going in a different direction. He's going from my right across my body, and then Mirandinha is running to my left towards the stands and Gibbo's chasing after him. Mirandinha jumped into the stands, and I thought "what's going on there" and the fella that I thought kicked me was Mirandinha's interpreter chasing him because he could see what he was about to do, so he was trying to stop him as he's booted me up the backside and legged it!'

This all sounds very comical, and typical Dons, but it could have got nasty. 'So he's in the fans and it's going off as a few of the players had gone to the stands. Then afterwards he'd obviously been told you can't do that. He was saying that he was disappointed because he'd always seen the FA Cup, and thought it was their year that they could win it. So, they made him come into our dressing room after the game and apologise. He went around and his understanding of the English language wasn't very good. He'd obviously been told what to say. "I'm sorry," coming round shaking everyone's hand saying "I'm sorry. I'm sorry," but because he didn't understand, a lot of our responses were with a smiley face but some expletives thrown in. But he just carried on. The irony was that at the end of the season after the final I signed for Newcastle, and I go up for my first day's training, as a new boy you get there early, are shown where you change and so on. Little did I know Mirandinha was always late, so all the players are in the dressing room and he comes in, his English is better now, "Big Dave! My friend." They put me and him next to each other.'

Watford in the quarter-final was a tie that saw change not only in that game, but for the rest of the season. 'Gayley was having a really good season and he got sent off. At the end of the game we're thinking, "Blimey, we're going to miss Gayley." He'd been that good, but the opportunity opened up for Eric Young. And he started playing so well that he stayed in. When the [semi-final] draw was being made, we were thinking we don't want Liverpool, we don't want [Nottingham] Forest, if only we can get Luton, we've got a chance. When the draw came out it was unbelievable, and then it was at White Hart Lane which was a ground where we liked going, as every time we went there, we seemed to do well. It was one that me personally, I used to like playing there. The way we arrived; it was typical Dons style. I lived in north-west London so Gouldy would say, "Right, we'll meet you at the ground, who's going straight there? You, you, you ..." About six made their own way to the ground on the day instead of on a coach. Gouldy drove the minibus with some of the lads on the bus and that's how we got to the semi-final of the cup. He [Gould] tells the story that they weren't letting them in, saying, "This isn't the team bus.'"

In big games you sometimes get the big speech, the rousing one that gets everyone hyped up and ready, but Beasant said there was no need for that. 'Johnny Giles was a columnist for the *Mail* or *Express*, or something, and he was really critical of us and said, "For the sake of football, Luton, you've got to win." He was hammering us, and Gouldy just put that write-up on the wall and said, "Read that. I don't need a team talk, read that." And that was it. I mean, we were out there to beat them anyway, but what Giles was saying and that it would be terrible for football for us to get to Wembley, and we shouldn't be allowed to play at Wembley, it wasn't right what he was saying. Before I signed for Wimbledon I played for Edgware Town, and so did Brian Stein, and he was now against me in the semi-final. He was up front with [Mick] Harford. You don't think, looking back, that two players playing non-league football would be against each other in a semi at White Hart Lane. [Dennis] Wise scored the two-footed goal that only he could score. He launched himself in and made sure that if one foot wouldn't get it two feet would. It was literally with the soles of his feet he pushed it in, and that was it. I can remember pictures of me carrying Wisey around. So we win the semi-final, and I don't think we won another game between that and the final, I think we drew most of the games.

'The focus was all on the final and the irony was we played Manchester United on the Monday. We went up there and its Gibbo's old club, and he said they're going to give us some. Normally if anyone wanted a fight we'd match them, and I can remember a couple of tackles going in early on, Bryan Robson and Gordon Strachan were saying, "You want to play in the final? I wouldn't come near me." It was the only time we lost a battle, and we lost up there 2-1. You knew why, as you didn't want to risk missing the final. Your mind was, "I've got to stay fit for the game, get through this and the final is next week."

'You can see why the focus drifts away from the league. We made a record, we wanted to do a remake of the "Wombles of Wimbledon", but this song, "We are Wimbledon", was written. We went to the iconic Abbey Road studios famous for the Beatles. As we're there the media are covering it as well and we said we want to do the Beatles thing on the zebra crossing. I think it was Vinnie, Fash, Gayle, Wise and myself. They held the traffic up a little bit so they can get the photo of us standing on the crossing like we're walking across it. The traffic is building up both ways and some fella has decided he's not going to wait in the queue. He's overtook and coming down the outside and we're on the crossing and he's just driving at us! As he's gone over and Fash and Vinnie were closest, and as it's gone by they just booted it, they gave it a proper boot. The car's stopped and we've gone back in the studio. The next thing is we've got the police at the studio door saying "we've got a report there's been a criminal act" so we told them what happened and they were like, "Oh, so he was overtaking on the crossing and didn't stop? Thank you very much, you've got nothing to worry about, I'll go and have a word with the driver." I think he let the driver off but the back of his car was all dented. I think he learned the consequences of what he shouldn't be doing.'

Doing an FA Cup Final song was a tradition in the 1980s, as was all the build-up to the game that made celebrities of the players. It was something they just weren't used to but had to get the hang of. 'So we done the song early on, then we had our suits done at Top Shop. Then *The Clothes Show* with Jeff Banks. They decided they would do an episode where we're going to be featured in our suits at the ground. No one else is there, and there's photos of me leaning against a goalpost, coat over the shoulder. Some of the lads were on the terrace, so it was like a fashion walk, and all the partners in their final dresses as well. Then you'd have your open training day to the media. They were in filming and families were involved, and that's where John Motson pulled me and said, "John Aldridge has never missed a penalty, and there's never been a penalty saved in the final. If there's a penalty, what will you do?"

'As much as people were critical of Wimbledon we were quite forward in our thinking. We had a fella called Vince Craven who used to do a lot of match analysis. When teams had been on TV he'd clip it all together and show it. Little clips and things, and the lads got bored watching it sometimes, but other times it was really informative. I'd seen Liverpool a few times on TV, they were mainly on *The Big Match* and *Match of the Day* every week, so we'd see them a lot. When they did have a penalty, I'd seen four or five of them, so I got to study a bit of his [Aldridge's] technique, so I said to Motson my thought process was that if they get one he does this little stutter, and if I can stay still through that stutter then he's got to strike the ball. He favoured going to the goalie's left but what normally happens is as he comes up and does that, the goalkeeper commits, and he puts it the opposite way, he leaves it that late to do it. A bit like the modern-day player does it, so when it all comes about and you hear the commentary, and he's saying, "I spoke to Dave in the week and if Aldridge gets a penalty ..." He's more or less talking you through it. But he's put that down as one of his iconic commentary moments, in his top five, the fact that he had pre-empted what was going to happen.'

It was almost the day of the game, and with all the excitement throughout the week, it was time to try and unwind. Something, again, that was unusual for a Dons trip away. 'It was in the Cannizaro Hotel, a nice hotel on the Common and we'd had our meal. I think Gouldy could sense the lads were getting edgy and he said, "What would you normally do?" We'd normally go in the bar and have a beer we told him, "Go on then." He says he gave us money but that's a lie, he never gave us any. So we went out to the pub just around the corner, and it's strange how things come together as the pub was the one that was used as the dressing room when the team played on the Common. The scene in the pub, it was like the westerns when you walk in the door, when the gunslinger walks in and the music stops. There were some fans in there with a bit of singing, but we all come in and it just stopped and they were like, "You got a final tomorrow!" We went in, usually me and Sanch would have a Guinness, Thorny and Cork a beer, Fash and Carlton an orange juice as they didn't drink, but we all went together and if you wanted one OK, if you don't fine, it was just to steady the nerves and stop yourself thinking. You can use up a lot of nervous energy, so it was about not thinking about the game, even though you're talking with a few fans and having a laugh it wasn't you're on your own thinking about the game. We just had a couple of beers and that was it, back to the hotel, in bed.'

Nine

Date With Destiny

FOR YEARS, decades, a worldwide television audience would tune in to Wimbledon. Each summer the fabled strawberries and cream would be devoured. The finely cut grass on the lawns of the All England Club would take centre stage on the aptly named Centre Court, as well as the surrounding ones. The name Wimbledon in sport is synonymous with tennis. It is that simple. Even those in London would know it as the home of the racket sport, and to be fair the town centre does pride itself on that fact. Why not? A year-round tourist attraction that for two weeks every year transforms itself into a hub of sporting excellence still regarded by most players as the one major tournament they would most like to win. In short, Wimbledon means tennis.

On 14 May 1988 there was a shift. It wasn't one that ripped apart the fabric of the town, but it certainly made people realise that there was more than just players wearing all white who would flash their brilliance for a fortnight and move on. There were streams of blue and yellow, and shouts from fans who could be more vocal than those sitting calmly, heads swaying side to side watching a game. Another corner of Wimbledon had its own heroes, and they played practically all year round. Tennis now had an annoying little sibling that it had to tolerate, but one that the town could show off and be proud of.

The football club had been around for just about as long as the tennis had been, and those who followed the football may not have a care for those who followed tennis. There was always room for both, and there had to be, as now the world knew about the football team, not just the locals, and those in British football also had to learn to live with the little sibling that had now grown up into a loud and brash young adult. It was fine to be in the shadow of the behemoth that visited once a year, like an overbearing reminder of who was biggest and trying to put you in your place, because once that had gone, football was still there. It would carry on reminding you that it wasn't going to go away.

When Bobby Gould walked out at Wembley, leading his line of tracksuited players out into the bright sunshine just before 3pm, the landscape changed for him and his players, staff, fans and the town. He couldn't have been any prouder. The fans couldn't have been louder, and in contrast, the doubters couldn't have been any quieter. This was it. The season had been long, the FA Cup run full of fun and tense moments, and the build-up finally over. There was a game to play. Gould and coach Don Howe had done all they could to get the players ready, both in body and mind. They just had to apply themselves, and not let the occasion get the better of them.

It's always guaranteed that on FA Cup Final day the sun will shine, almost an unwritten rule in football, and this day in particular proved that to be true. The sun was high and would be at its hottest at the start of the game, and temperatures did not cool down, creating the hottest day of the year. Would tempers stay cool was a question that was answered in the opening ten minutes as Vinnie Jones clattered into Steve McMahon. It was a statement that simply said, 'We're here, and we'll be here all afternoon.'

It was hard to tell if that challenge had an impact across the whole Liverpool team, as the sabre-rattling had already started in the tunnel before the teams started the long walk out into the arena with Jones leading a chorus of tribalistic chanting that was part to hype themselves up, as well as get into the heads of their opponents. It was going to be hard to rattle Liverpool in this way though, as their players had been into many hostile stadiums abroad in the past for club or country, so they had pretty much been there and done that. But this was a domestic final, where decorum was usually at play. Wimbledon were a different breed and snarled their way up the tunnel, not with a disrespect for where they were but more keeping in tune with who they were. 'Yidaho!' was the battle cry.

'We were all shouting and hollering, but everyone remembers Vinnie more than most. He spits when he shouts,' said John Fashanu when he looked back at the tunnel antics. Jones explained the origins as something that came from him and his mates when they did something great. He had offered tickets to all his Watford pals, but they said the real fans should get them, so in a way the chant went up as a homage to them, 'Fash and Wisey joined in and then everyone else. And once we won, we couldn't stop shouting it.' Dennis Wise was part of it all but admitted that he wasn't sure what to do at first, 'I had no idea what it's usually like down there, whether you are supposed to be quiet and well mannered, but we weren't going to change our pre-match routine.'

The challenge on McMahon didn't get a booking, nor a real talking to. Referee Brian Hill had probably been waiting for that moment so, unless it was completely reckless, he would take a mental note instead. 'That was our mark on the game, it said that no one was going to come through the middle,' Terry Phelan remarked. As expected, Liverpool had lots of early possession, but the Dons would carry a threat at set pieces and had the first real chance of the game. Shortly after Alan Cork had got smartly ahead of John Aldridge in the first moments to clear the ball over from a John Barnes cross, Wimbledon went up the other end and Wise had a free kick 20 yards out just left of centre. His effort was well struck but dipped too late and may well have drifted wide too. Peter Beardsley was the real threat, popping up around the box, weaving his runs, staying elusive, and he found Ray Houghton on the right. The former Oxford player drove into the box and pulled back a cross into the path of Aldridge who didn't connect properly and with Beasant on the floor, already committed to stopping the first shot, the goalkeeper managed to claw the ball away with Barnes odds-on to get an easy tap-in. Jones, who had spotted the danger from his midfield position, thrashed it away for a corner. It was a chance, but dogged determination had prevailed.

Wimbledon came alive and started to play their own football. A move that involved Fashanu bringing the ball forward to the left and exchanging with Lawrie Sanchez led to Cork drifting in towards the penalty spot where a centre was aimed. Cork couldn't win the header but the loose ball carried over to the left side of the box where Wise was in acres of space. He was soon chased down by three defenders, such was his threat, but not before he swept the ball over again and it was met with a half-volley on the edge of the box by Fashanu, whose spinning shot was just inches wide.

Just after the half hour mark came one of the most talked-about decisions of the game, a real turning point and a let-off for the Dons. They say you earn your luck, so perhaps this was the moment all the hard work paid off.

Beardsley was sent away with a 30-yard pass from the back by Alan Hansen, and he collected the ball in his stride just over the halfway line. Andy Thorn was in close attendance and the two went shoulder-to-shoulder, the defender tugging the attacker's shirt, the player in red staying upright as the one in blue fell to the ground. A roar went up as Beardsley advanced with just Beasant to beat, and a faint whistle could be heard. This didn't stop Beardsley, no doubt deafened by the expectant crowd, and he dinked the ball over Beasant and started to celebrate. Nobody was joining in though, already aware that the referee had pulled play back for a foul by Thorn. The Liverpool players were incensed that play wasn't allowed to continue and that the goal had been chalked off. Wimbledon breathed a sigh of relief, while Bruce Grobbelaar just huffed, 'If he [the referee] had been fit, he would have been up with the play when Beardsley put the ball in the net. He should have given Peter the advantage, instead he penalised us.'

Moments later, Phelan was in an advanced position on the left and had Steve Nicol pulling at his arm as the two ran to the goal line near the corner flag. 'Howe had told us to head out wide and look for the overlaps and if we could get free kicks, we would get them. Liverpool were terrified of us in the air,' Phelan said. The linesman raised his flag and a free kick was awarded. Wise came over from his right-sided position to take it. A queue of alternate team players formed on the six-yard line before a perfectly flighted ball was sent over, and Sanchez got the deftest of flicks to keep Grobbelaar rooted to the ground and watching as the ball nestled into the far corner. Set pieces were always going to be the biggest opportunity for the Dons to score, and Liverpool clearly hadn't done their homework. The Reds had one more big chance to level the scores before half-time when Hansen was the highest up the pitch he'd been all game and played a lovely one-two with Houghton on the edge on the box, but Beasant was alert and came out to block the shot and preserve the lead.

With fresh shirts and ice-cold towels, the half-time team talk was more of a chill-out zone, but Thorn recalled Howe's measured lines among all the chatter, 'Don't sit back, don't start wasting time, keep playing the way you are and you'll win this.' Within moments of the second half, Jones had hacked a clearance. The message was understood.

Liverpool would keep probing and with Barnes being nullified with some cute tactics by Howe, and well executed by Wise and Clive Goodyear, it was Beardsley who was pulling the strings. His own wall pass with Aldridge on the hour allowed the Irish striker an opening in the box but a retreating Goodyear stretched his leg out to knock the ball away from his path just as it seemed the shot would be fired. Beasant claimed the ball, but the whistle had gone. Hill had seen the tumbling Aldridge and thought the only way he would have gone down was if he had been fouled. Aldridge got up sheepishly; he hadn't conned the referee with dramatics, but maybe he knew he had got away with one, and as he got ready to take the spot kick it was Wimbledon who were now feeling wronged by the official. Maybe the referee was trying to atone for the error of not continuing play earlier and letting the Beardsley goal stand. It was something on Phelan's mind, 'My veins were pumping and there must have been 80,000 Scousers in the stadium all mad for it.' The ball had been clearly won as first Phelan, then Young and Goodyear protested, but it was the captain who pulled them back to stop anything worse happening. After realising he had his own job to do,, Beasant retreated to his line. No goalkeeper had saved a penalty in an FA Cup Final. Records are meant to be broken; Beasant dived to his left and with a strong push the ball went wide. History had been made.

The match still had more than 20 minutes left but everyone was starting to get the feeling it would be the underdogs' day. In search of the goal to seal the win, Wise, still buzzing about, sent a cross from the right which Fashanu headed over from 12 yards. 'I was physically and mentally exhausted. I couldn't move. I had cramp in both legs and I was praying that the game would end. I have never experienced such pain before,' Fash admitted, and for him to be feeling it, the occasion must have been debilitating. 'I was getting delirious from the heat,' Thorn confirmed. 'We kept asking the referee how long was left and he kept saying "not long", but how long is not long!'

Beardsley then fed Gary Ablett in the left channel and his pacy cross was headed wide by Barnes. The chances were drying up, and ones that were being created were not finished off. Proof of that was when a rare Wimbledon corner from Wise again came to Young on the edge of the box. The towering centre-back was used to heading towards goal, not striking the ball, but this was a fair attempt on target, and Grobbelaar saved well. Then in the dying moments with Liverpool throwing everything forward, Nicol headed over substitute Jan Mølby's long throw. Another throw halfway up the Wimbledon half of the field was sent in, but as it landed referee Hill blew the whistle. The first person to shake his hand was Vinnie Jones. Then it was just chaos with Thorn jumping on Beasant's back, Cork and Sanchez hugging, Fashanu's clenched fists punching the air, Gould and Howe with arms around each other's shoulders, and just a general sense of overwhelming relief and happiness. Even Princess Diana was suppressing a wide smile.

After the players gathered together they went up to collect the cup, Beasant leading the line as only the second goalkeeper to captain a side in the final, Wise filing up behind him. At this point everyone was running on adrenaline but living all their childhood dreams out. Scenes they had watched on their televisions over many years, but ones that when plying their trade in lower-league football they could never had dreamed possible, were now a reality playing out in front of millions worldwide. The cup was handed over by the Princess of Wales, followed by handshakes and smiles from the captain, before he turned and lifted it high with a couple of loud shouts towards where the Dons fans were waiting, most still in disbelief but enjoying every single moment with their team. 'We'd done it. As a kid you try to imagine what it must feel like, and here I was, and it was happening. It just didn't sink in. I thank Gould and Howe for telling us to take our time walking around at the end as it may not happen again. They were right,' said Phelan of that lap of honour that took an age.

Having received their medals after the Wimbledon players had come back down the other side of the steps, Liverpool were off the pitch quickly and conducting their interviews. 'Wimbledon played to their strength, and we didn't play to ours. We were going to pull off Aldridge but being the penalty taker he stayed on until then,' Dalglish lamented to the press, and his captain Hansen was also stoic: 'We were always going to be under pressure as the favourites. Now we will be meeting Wimbledon again in the Charity Shield in August. Things might be different then.' Wimbledon would be in the press rooms soon, but not until after they had the obligatory group photoshoot, the whole staff jigging and singing as the large bank of media snapped shots that would soon be seen in newspapers and magazines. The lap of honour was special, as each player took turns holding the trophy and some revelled in it more than others, Jones in particular swinging it around as he bellowed to mates in the crowd. As they approached the area where the television studios were perched high up, some players would point to their former boss, Dave Bassett. He was grinning as much as the players as they acknowledged his part in their success. It was a touching moment, as this group remained grounded enough to know where they came from and who helped them on this incredible journey.

In the small media room, the winners arrived; cameras all around them, the world still watching. The ITV and BBC interviewers were ready for them. Jim Rosenthal and Tony Gubba, ever the professionals, gathered among the Crazy Gang. They were conducting their live broadcasts next to each other and so the cheers went up from both groups when replays were being shown. It all seemed a bit rushed considering the hours of build-up but then who wants to stand around chatting when there's celebrating to do? 'Alan Cork, you tell me you have enjoyed going to work every day for the last ten years, you must have enjoyed today?' asked Rosenthal. 'I've had a right good day today,' Cork replied. 'I got dragged off though – I was breathing out my backside.' Showing his medal off to the camera and to his former boss watching on as part of the ITV broadcast team upstairs, he continued, 'I'm still shaking, look. I'm going to wake up tomorrow and look at this and realise I've won a medal, first time in my life.'

Alongside Cork was Clive Goodyear, with Beasant in the background. Rosenthal managed to ask about the penalty while showing the incident to the group. Goodyear said, 'Well yeah, I thought I won the ball cleanly, he over-run the ball, and I managed to get a toe in to get it away from him, so a bit disappointed but the big fella did brilliant.' At which point Beasant leant over and laughed, jokingly saying, 'He said he'd make me a hero one day. We took on the best in the country and beat them, so we must be close to second best.' The odds on a Wimbledon win were 4/1 and everyone was asked if they'd taken up anyone on that bet. 'I had £20 on it with the local bookmaker!' called out Eric Young. No one had heard Young up until this point so that was some light relief in itself. Then on the left John Fashanu appeared, so Rosenthal continued with his questions and asked the top scorer for his thoughts on those who had said it would be bad for football in the Dons won, the critics. Fashanu replied, 'Nobody gave us any hope. The critics – we read about it every day. Johnny Giles and [national newspaper journalist] Jeff Powell. I can't read though, none of us can read, we just look at the pictures.'

Tony Gubba had the job for the BBC of trying to get some sensible words out of the boisterous Dons players after the game, and at first he had Sanchez, Wise and Jones in front of him, turning straight to the goalscorer with a monitor handy to show the magical moment back to them. Jones immediately joked that he couldn't remember who scored the goal, but Sanchez soon reminded them all, 'I score one or two, but I only score the important ones. I got one at Huddersfield to put us up and I suppose this one is quite important today as well. Just a glancing header, I had a special haircut today as well, so it worked.'

It was hard to contain Jones as he whooped upon seeing the replay, but Gubba would come to him soon enough, as first he turned to Wise and the statistic of him being involved in 75 per cent of Wimbledon goals. 'There it is, that's all I can say,' Wise said cheekily. 'That's our usual free kick so I'm surprised teams don't defend it better,' Sanchez said when another angle of the goal was flashed up.

Attention then turned to Jones, who was asked about how Wimbledon stopped the usual way Liverpool played. He responded, 'We was told it would be a battle for the midfield and it surely was, but there was another nine players out there. It's just a brilliant day, I'm happy for the lads back home watching in the pubs.' This was vintage Vinnie, if there was such a thing as his career was still quite new, and when the 'scars' on him were pointed out he said, 'Yeah, you should see the other boys, the boys in the red.' It was of course typical Vinnie and Wise again had that impish grin.

'Clive's taken the ball'; 'He's won the ball'; 'Never a penalty', the three chirped as the penalty incident was shown to them. 'But Dave has to have his moment, he likes to save a penalty every now and again,' added Sanchez.

Wise recalled the research on Aldridge, 'We watched them before on the box taking a penalty against Forest, he checked, then he played it.' The Aldridge penalty was shown and Sanchez said, 'Good penalty, great save. One of the best goalkeepers in the country, what can you do against him?' And right on cue, Beasant walked in having completed the ITV media call, 'I just tried to stand up. He goes a lot to the keeper's left and I just tried to stand still. He didn't do his shuffle; he didn't do his stop and start and I'm disappointed as I should have caught it.' Again this typified the Wimbledon spirit.

The focus shifted then to those who made things tick. Sam Hammam was called into line and the cup thrust into his hands, and the players were ribbing him, but he was used to it and openly let the jokes flow over him but was relieved when his manager, with his coach, joined the conversation. The calm and precise Don Howe said, 'We worked at it, we spent two hours yesterday afternoon, a lot of people wouldn't have done that, they'd have been saving their legs. But we worked at it for two hours, they filled their time in, and they've played it out superbly, and I couldn't have asked for anything better. I know Liverpool were on top of us in the second half but they never really created a chance and I don't think it was a penalty either.'

When it was put to Bobby Gould how the team had managed to slow Liverpool down, he turned it more on to how his players had fared, 'We're in a position of believing in our ability, and knowing that we've scored a lot of goals from dead-ball situations, and as the master next to me [Howe] said, they worked yesterday afternoon. People were looking at us, and we're still out working at ten to six last night, and for anybody to think that you can't work before a cup final, you see what we thought is you give them too much time this lot, they have too much time to think. So we're in a situation where we're working on a very warm afternoon, and I think, I know, that helped them through today.'

Howe was then asked about the critics, and how they had put Wimbledon down before a ball had even been kicked. He reflected, 'For some unknown reason, I think, it's a little bit, kind of people look down their nose at people that want to graft, and we're a terrific example to the rest of football. There is room at the top. It shouldn't be Manchester United, Liverpool, all these teams every year, but to hear a lot of people talk that's all they want and that's wrong, that's not how things should be. People from the bottom should be able to get to the top.'

In a last biting speech, Gould responded to a comment about the match being a grafting final. 'Tony,' he commanded, 'do you expect us to come here just to please you, the media? Because we don't come here to please you, we come here to win, and we grafted and we won. We've worked since we were at home to West Bromwich Albion, at Mansfield, at Newcastle, against Watford, at Luton. We worked, Tony, and that's the name of the game and this is sheer perspiration, just as you're sweating Tony 'cos it's hard work. But we're going to enjoy it, we're going to enjoy every moment, and to all the viewers back home thanks for watching us, and to the media,' he continued, breaking off for a nod and a smile to the camera. 'We did it!'

Ten

End of an Era

'I HOPE you're enjoying yourself. We're going to get drunk! See you next season.'

Dave Beasant, hero of the hour, practically on the hour, shouted down to the gathered masses waiting below him, clad in and waving anything yellow and blue.

It was a scene that was picture perfect for Wimbledon fans, but one that even looking back seems as far-fetched than any fairy tale, as it was being called. Sure, it is a story that could be dreamed up by scriptwriters and storytellers, with an ending that would even have avid readers of *Roy of the Rovers* scratching their heads. The players took their turns holding the cup aloft, each one greeted by a huge cheer, and chairman Stanley Reed started his traditional sing-along, 'Here we are again ... happy as can be.' Each player was nursing a hangover of some description, or defying aching limbs and tired eyes, but at this stage the sheer adulation and adrenaline took over. It didn't matter how sore they were, the aches would wait another few hours to be tended to; in fact let's wait another couple of days. Why not, we've earned it, right?

'Last week we thought we would need rent-a-crowd if we won. But we are thrilled with the turnout today,' a beaming Bobby Gould said. His side had defied the odds. Those who had chosen to lay down any hard-earned cash at those generous prices would be making their way to the bookmakers, if they hadn't cashed in already, and coming back with a healthy return. Gould needn't have worried though, even if when the Official London Tours Sightseeing open-top bus pulled away with just a few people walking along the pavements. Surely after one of football's greatest moments there would be more than a pram-pushing mother on her way to the shop, or the elderly couple walking their dog, looking up at the players as they raced to their destination of the Town Hall in the centre of the high street.

To be fair, most parades start off slow; those helping the organising of it all were the ones who started things off, seeing the bus on its way and then following behind. But seeing as the fanbase wasn't big, unlike Liverpool who still had a parade planned and attended by twice as many as they showed off their only silverware in the shape of the league title, expectation was low.

'We're just little Wimbledon, no one cares about us,' John Scales thought. Slowly though there were more people heading in the general direction the bus was – to the town. A corner was turned and a sea of flags and scarves opened up before the players' eyes. Fashanu did not drink so was able to take the moment in clearly and was glad he did, 'I couldn't believe it. None of us could. The whole of Wimbledon was a sea of yellow and blue.'

Inside the Town Hall the winners were greeted by the mayor, and other luminaries, including Angela Rumbold, the junior education minister, sporting a blue dress with a yellow flower pinned on it. Andy Thorn had a quick look around and spotted something, 'It turned out the mayor had a bar in his chambers. So we went through that too.' Alan Cork was one of those feeling the worse for wear, 'I was just sitting at the back of the bus with sunglasses on. I could barely bloody move. But the drinking just carried on, all the way through the reception, at the Town Hall, and on to my testimonial.'

As the team retreated back inside from the balcony, with its hastily thrown-together bunting, the crowd started to drift away. The buzz of excitement was still in the air as fans told their own stories of how the previous day's events had unfolded. Then some had to carefully get down from their lofty perches on lamp-posts. It's easier to get down them than up, though, so that was some relief for them.

It had always been planned, and now it was extra special. Cork was in his testimonial year, and he could not have planned this any better. He was the self-confessed grump of the side, although he would say that Lawrie Sanchez was a close second. He deserved this moment; his loyal service was being repaid. Would the estimated 25,000 who turned up at lunchtime the day before all be there at Plough Lane and make this an even bigger celebration? No one was banking on that, and so on a balmy evening the gates opened for the last time in the season. In the end the crowd was still healthy with just over 7,000 paying close to £20,000 in gate receipts, and with other areas of income it was a healthy payday for the player who had been a bargain free transfer a decade before. The night was due to involve two games of football – a veterans' match with Dave Bassett back to coax a side into action, with Bobby Gould keeping an eye on his selected team, then a Wimbledon XI against a London XI. The proceedings were delayed for close to an hour though as a special guest made an appearance, a bigger celebrity or star than any invited guest.

The FA Cup.

Cork game out to a huge cheer, and while holding the trophy he had the broadest grin that anyone had ever seen on him. This was breaking character and it was a joy to see. The main game played out with the usual quirks that grace such occasions, the primary one being the role reversal of Terry Gibson and Dave Beasant swapping positions, and it's still a question as to which looked the more bizarre – the tiny figure of Gibson in goal or the towering one of Beasant in open play. Then in a further switch Vinnie Jones went in goal, and to add to the jovial atmosphere Cork scored an own goal to end the scoring at 2-2. The result didn't matter, no one cared really, but for the record Cork scored at both ends with Sanchez suitably getting the other for Wimbledon, and Ian Wright scoring the other London XI goal.

The game will always be remembered for the 'bum salute' that the players gave the baying crowd. It started off harmlessly enough, with a chorus from the terraces of 'Vinnie, show us your bum', although he was reluctant to do so if teasing a little bit. After some cajoling of his team-mates, an organised line was made and all the players slipped down the back of their shorts, revealing their bare cheeks. It was all done in jest and no harm was done, except it was caught on camera. Gould had seen what was happening before it did but was helpless to stop it, and when the picture surfaced after the *Daily Mirror* acquired it, another FA charge was on the way. Not a great end to the season or start to the new one, and things were only to get worse.

It was inevitable really that some players' heads would be turned. Clubs had seen how well they could perform under pressure, and the Dons' stars were now names who people knew and rated. The team would start to break up and Gould would have to rebuild certain areas. The biggest loss was a double swoop by Newcastle United when they signed both Dave Beasant and Andy Thorn, for £850,000 each. Clearly it was a case of if you can't beat them, sign them. Then another defensive stalwart left, Brian Gayle moving to Manchester City for £350,000. Players were asking for more money, and the harmony of the team was being disrupted, and with several out injured the team that took to the field against Liverpool in the Charity Shield to start the season was fundamentally different. Simon Tracey made his debut in goal. So long an understudy to Beasant, he now had his time, as did Peter Cawley, who stepped in at centre-back with both Thorn and Gayle – who had competed all year – gone. Carlton Fairweather was back from his leg break and came into the midfield with Vaughan Ryan, replacing Cork and Jones. John Scales was in at right-back for the injured Clive Goodyear. Andy Clement and Robbie Turner would make substitute appearances. It was a complete shift but looked like business as usual when Dennis Wise crossed for John Fashanu to thump home a header after just 17 minutes but the day was on a different spectrum to the one in May; it rained, the attendance was short of 55,000, and Wimbledon lost. And John Aldridge redeemed himself by getting both goals, the first after Tracey made a mess of a clearance, as Liverpool came back to win.

Tracey would play once more for Wimbledon, on the opening day of the 1988/89 league season against Arsenal on a baking-hot afternoon in London. Plough Lane had almost 16,000 packed in as the FA Cup winners welcomed the later-to-be First Division champions. Fashanu scored again, another big header inside ten minutes, but soon after that Tracey dropped Brian Marwood's cross and the ball went in for an equaliser. From there the Gunners dominated and were 3-1 up at half-time, eventually winning 5-1.

It would be harsh to say the end of an era had been reached; Gould made some astute signings and Wimbledon went on to finish 12th, but didn't threaten the top positions and were thankful for a good run after Christmas that saw them move away from the relegation spots. In their defence of the FA Cup they beat Birmingham City at St Andrew's by a single Terry Gibson goal after half an hour, then won by the same score at Villa Park when Jones scored on the hour to knock out Aston Villa. The 'Harry the Haddock' game as it's known – it seemed like every other visiting fan brought with them an inflatable fish, such was the terrace craze for inflatables that season – was the fifth-round tie at home to Grimsby Town, and after the visitors took a shock lead, three second-half goals by Fashanu, Phelan, and Wise put the Dons through to the last eight.

A few weeks before they were due to play Everton in the quarter-final, they faced the Toffees in the First Division at Goodison. Vinnie Jones was sent off after getting too close to Kevin Ratcliffe in a heated confrontation that the referee adjudged to be a head-butt. The game would end 1-1, but the Goodison Park faithful would not forget, and a stadium that can create a hostile environment at the best of times was now a cauldron. Colin Harvey tried to play the situation down, saying, 'It's quite possible people will be looking in today for the wrong reason. But as far as we're concerned, and I'm sure Wimbledon would agree with me, it's just another day, another game.'

Jones started the cup tie on the bench and was a target for abuse. Hans Segers was now Wimbledon's established goalkeeper, and he saved a tame Graeme Sharp penalty to keep dreams of retaining the FA Cup alive. This game was just like Mansfield and Newcastle rolled into one, but with half an hour to go Stuart McCall struck the only goal to knock the Dons out in front of a live Sunday afternoon television audience. It had been a valiant attempt to retain the cup, but they came across a team that wanted it more, through past encounters, and had revenge on their minds. Everton were just too much on that day and the dream was over. 'To be honest Everton mugged us off at our own game. We pride ourselves with a will-to-win and discipline, but Everton were the only side that showed that,' said Lawrie Sanchez, unable to mask his disappointment. For Gould it was also hard to disguise his thoughts, but he decided to offer little to the press straight after the game, 'We were not good enough. Full marks to Everton, I wish them well. Goodnight gentlemen.'

Wimbledon had their day though, that glorious one on 14 May 1988. It will never be forgotten, by those who were there, both playing and watching. It was a day that John

Motson, the man whose voice on the BBC's broadcasts of the FA Cup Final was as guaranteed as it was to have the game be played on a hot day, came up with two lines that will always be immortalised by Dons fans, and sum up the whole story.

'The Crazy Gang have beaten the Culture Club,' is the first that everyone will recall, but the best one that captures everything that the whole club is about, with its fans too:

'It's a weird and wonderful world if you come from Wimbledon!'

The Captain's Story – Part Two
Dave Beasant

'IN THE morning you get up and the papers are around and you're doing the things you've seen other teams doing. The cameras are there, Uncle Bulgaria was there [one of the Wombles, if you're unsure], we had a cup final agent, Eric Hall, saying, "You got to have this paper under your arm, and you got to have this can of drink in your hand." We had two buses. A team bus, and one was for the wives. They'd come to the hotel to say goodbye, they didn't stay with us, just came to see us off. Then off we went on the journey you see so often, the helicopter above seeing the bus on the road, and a camera team on the bus doing the odd interview on the way. But it was just like the journey to any other game – you'd play cards, others watching the TV.

'Going to Wembley is like my backyard. I grew up in Willesden, and my first house was in

Kingsbury, which is why I could see the twin towers on the way to training. I was giving a guided tour on the way there, "Go over there, that's where I drink sometimes, that's where I used to play football." We get to Wembley and we're coming down Wembley Way and we can hardly see a blue and yellow flag or scarf. It was all red and white everywhere. Because we're local we're going to arrive late, but their fans were down early on the train, but it was a sea of red and white.

'When the bus came to the tunnel, at the big gates, I could see outside the window and my brother was there. He was holding my young son Nick, at the time he was two and a half, and my other son was born on the eve of the Luton game. On the Thursday night I was in hospital until about 4am and the nurse didn't take too favourably to me staying. I nicked a couple of pillows and slept on the floor, and was asleep until the early hours, then went into training late. The lads trained in the morning, and me in the afternoon. Fash stayed late and we were doing penalty training together. Anyway, my brother was at the side of the bus and the surge pushed him against the side of it with my lad, and I'm hoping they're all right. We get off the bus in the tunnel with the gates shut. As I got off, he's there with my son. Because he was crying the police said let him in to see his dad, then they took them out, so it was good to see them both in the tunnel at Wembley.

'You know how much it meant in those days. We'd all seen these great players playing cup finals and I think we wanted to savour it. It might be our only chance so we were going to enjoy the day. We're going to enjoy it by winning first and foremost, but everything about it, all the stuff we'd seen, we are going to be doing that. Seeing where your family are before the game and waving at them, then the interviews on the pitch, but once you know you're coming off the pitch, you know you're getting ready to work. In dressing rooms with the really deep bath that you could literally stand up in, and then you just go into preparation mode. Have a laugh and the music started going, I can remember I'd always have to shoot off to the loo before games – you couldn't go out and warm up before the final like you normally would, because of the marching bands – I could hear "Abide With Me" and I stayed in the loo a bit longer as that's when it hit me and I got a bit nervous. But it was good nerves, excitement.

'A lot is made of us coming into the tunnel with them. We were in the dressing room, and we always do things and geeing each other up. Liverpool had come out before us, and were all vocal, and they look over at us thinking, "What the hell we got here?" Some say we psyched them out in the tunnel. I wouldn't say anything like that, we were ourselves. Wembley was just another day of the week to them, whereas it was a big thing for us.'

The club had known about Princess Diana being the royal guest of honour, and a cheeky plan was hatched on the morning of the game, 'Vinnie and Fash were planning on giving her a bouquet of flowers, but we all said, "It isn't about you, we're here to do a job, you aren't taking those out," but it made the day even more special to us with her there. When she did the walk out to meet the players, she did Liverpool first, then came to me and said, "You're a big lad." Quick thinking, I replied, "I thought you'd have done your homework and put some high heels on." She said, "Well if I put heels on I'd be sinking in the soil, so I couldn't." Then I can't remember what I'm saying as I introduce her to all the players, and that's it, and off you go. We have a kick-around, Corky would always warm me up, and I can remember thinking, "I'm not going to let him score." I'm consciously thinking, "Corky, just hit my hands, don't try and beat me, hit my hands. I want you to work me, and the ball's not going in my net today."

'The best decision Gould made was to bring Don Howe in,' added Beasant. The England coach was seen as a hard taskmaster, but a pleasant surprise awaited the players. 'We were sceptical at first, thinking, "He's coming from the Arsenal and he's going to expect things, and be disgusted by the way we were," but on the first day of training, I can't remember the joke he told, and when the punchline came out and he was "right, here we go" and we're all thinking, "Blimey, he's all right, him." He then started, "We might not look like Brazil, but we're going to play like Brazil in our warm-ups," and we're going to be shoulder up, shoulder down, when jogging. Brazilian warm-ups were all in rhythm, stretching right to left like that, and he got us regimental in the way we warmed up. All sequenced, and it was quite a laugh. His tactics for the final were on John Barnes, player of the year that year, outstanding. So Don put Wise on the right, "You can run all day and we need you to double up and help Clive [Goodyear] to prevent Barnes being a threat."'

Beasant can remember the two notable moments from his point of view that were crucial in the eventual win. 'Thorn fouled him, and I heard the whistle,' he said of the moment the referee called play back after Peter Beardsley was impeded, 'but like I said I don't care, the ball's not going in, but instead of just letting him through I'm thinking he isn't getting through, but when he dinked it over me, I'm gutted. But I knew it wasn't a goal as I heard the whistle, which you can just hear on the TV too.'

The first real moment of drama though was almost out of reach. '[Ray] Houghton came in on the right,' said Beasant, then Houghton's cut-back went to his team-mate, 'and Aldridge didn't hit it cleanly, but I'd already started to dive to my left. It hit Eric Young's leg and went to my right, and it hit my leg and spun in the air. It was like it was on a string. I'm on my back looking up at this football and it just wouldn't come down. I can see Barnes coming in; for him it's not a tricky dribble or a wonder goal, he was going to tap it in from a yard. Just as he's jumping to volley it in, I've somehow got my go-go gadget arms up, Mark Morris used to say it was like the cartoon character Inspector Gadget, and claw it away. That save was more important than the penalty save because if they'd scored in the first half, we're up against it. We took the lead and got something to defend. It gave me a lot of confidence. I don't think the commentators realised I saved it, they didn't make much comment on it.'

With the lead and the half-time whistle blown, it was time for another masterstroke. 'We go in at half-time 1-0 up and Howe was throwing towels at us, soaked in the ice bucket. White Wembley towels. "Get them over your head and get your body temperature down quickly so you can focus." He learned that in Mexico in 1986 with England. So we've all got these towels on and Bobby's talking, and I've lifted mine up to have a look and it was a comical sight. You couldn't see faces, it was just everyone covered in a white towel. Gould was saying his piece and I've no idea what he said. It wasn't one of those riveting talks that was going to mean something to us, we were just all under the towels. Funny.'

Next was Beasant's big moment, even though it should never have come about. It's now firmly in the Dons' history. 'In those days you didn't have diving, and he didn't dive,' was Beasant's fair assessment of Aldridge earning the penalty. 'He's come across Clive from right to left, and Clive's facing me. He just toed it to me and Aldridge has not been able to stop, and [referee] Brian Hill gave it. I jumped up and everyone was after him. I said, "Leave it to me. I'll sort it," but I'm thinking he isn't going to change his mind. It was the most energy I've exerted chasing the ref and I've got to get my breath back before facing the penalty. I wasn't aware but they were getting ready to take him [Aldridge] off as he wasn't having a great game. Commentary said it was lucky they kept him on as he's the penalty taker, and I'm thinking the same as I've no idea where the other takers would have gone.' That strange twist of fate again. 'Thorny and Wisey were in his ear, "miss, miss, he's going to save it" as much as they could do. You see his face, he doesn't look that confident, but he struck it well, but it's where I thought so I was pushing and if it were a yard outside the post, I'd have still reached it as I had all that adrenaline and energy. I felt I could do anything; two hands pushed it around the post. Fash jumped in front of me and I'm trying to organise, and he's on his knees at my feet! Then the corner, Barnes puts it in at the near post, and no one was there so I thought this is a piece of cake, and I've dropped it, but I've fallen back on it. It was a good thing for me as I was treating the corner as easy, and that reminded me that the hard work wasn't done.'

The final whistle went while the Dons were under a bit more pressure, but facing no real chances of note. The tactics were played out to near perfection. 'Unbelievable. I went to get my glove bag I used to have from the sponsor, and Thorny jumped on my back. We were just walking around with him on my back, I looked, and people were cuddling on the floor here and there, others jumping around. The FA official came and got me and said,

"Will you take your boys together and go and get the trophy?" I went to Bruce [Grobbelaar] at the end of the game and he gave me a pair of sunglasses, they were two tennis rackets that overlapped. He jokingly said, "I was hoping to give these to you during the game." Maybe they were thinking they could be that dominant that he could come up for a corner. They were in a beige case, and I put them in my glove bag, and I said we'll swap shirts, he said OK. We go up and get the cup and people were giving us stuff. I got a hat and gave it to Wisey.

'I was always getting my hands damaged. I had my hands all strapped up. You could see the strapping and at the cup final they thought I'd started a new trend as keepers now always go and get the trophy with their gloves on showing the sponsor or manufacturer name. The fact was my left hand was quite strapped up; we didn't want people to see all the strapping on it so I had no glove on my right hand, but my left hand I kept the glove on so you couldn't see it all around my thumb and finger.

'I can't remember what Princess Diana said to us, but I did what every other cup captain does and showed it to our fans. Wisey behind was "oi oi, you bastards" right in front of Diana.'

Back down the 39 famous steps, and the team posed for the photos that were sent all around the world. 'Vinnie was so excited and Gouldy was telling us not to let ourselves down now with what's going on. The lap of honour was brilliant, it took us forever, and some Liverpool fans stayed and applauded us. But in front of our fans going round the sand of the old dog track, it was amazing. You suddenly realise what effort you'd put in to win the game, and in that heat worked your bollocks off to achieve it. So you sit down and take it in, then get ready for the journey home. Gouldy was sitting in front with the trophy next to the driver so everyone could see it. It was literally my journey to work every day, Hammersmith roundabout, down Fulham Road, over Putney Bridge.'

With the final won it was time to celebrate, and something had been long in the planning. 'The week after the semi-final, Stanley Reed and Sam Hammam spoke to me and asked, "What do you want to do after the cup final? Whatever the result, we can either go to the Hilton Park Lane, you and your partners and have a meal there, or we can have a marquee on the pitch at Plough Lane with a table for ten." Straight away we said on the pitch, that's the way we do things. We got back to the hotel and then on to Plough Lane. Our families come over. People think we must have gone mad that night, but we didn't. Everything had been taken out of you from the game. If we were at the Hilton, it would be the women together, and the lads together, and would have been quite lively. Whereas we had a table of ten with friends and family. We'd go to the bar with two or three of the lads together, have a chat then go back to them. It was more or less a sedate night in Dons terms, no Crazy Gang celebration throwing drinks over each other or getting naked. Gibbo was one of the last back, we had people shuttling us back to the hotel and he got back in a police van! After a quiet drink in the bar, we ordered every paper for the morning, and there was piles of papers outside each room. We wanted everything to do with it.'

After maybe a couple of hours' sleep everyone was up again for breakfast and then they headed to Wimbledon town centre. 'The open-top bus arrives, wives and partners with us. From the Common to tennis courts, then to Plough Lane. We're all on the top deck going 30mph, and we've got flies hitting us in the face, the wives' hair all blown everywhere. Around 200 people there, we're thinking, "This isn't going to go well, average home gate of 7,500, and we got 200 people here walking alongside us." A few more people down the side of the road, but not deep, going slowly and people walking alongside us. We get to the Village, and it's a bit busier, then we turn to the Town Hall and suddenly there's a mass of people. It was a relief as much as anything. It was a great sight to see. All the fans enjoying themselves, then on the balcony to show the trophy to them and say a few words and have a laugh.'

There was one more game to play, although it wasn't in an official capacity; Alan Cork's testimonial would end in more controversy. 'A very light-hearted affair,' said Beasant. 'I turned up an hour before and there were more beers in the dressing room. We go out and start playing, I think it was a Terry Venables London XI, the fans were in party spirit; a few chants of "Vinnie show us yer bum" then another player, and so on. Some would, some wouldn't, then we got to half-time and I said to the lads, "We can't bottle it, we'll all do it together." So we stood there in front of them and did a team moon. Cheers went up and someone took a photo. The next day it was in the *Daily Mirror*, and it was "look what they're doing now", and it was a spot the ball, "and for anyone who's not got a dirty mind its under Phelan's foot". You could literally say, "There's Bes 'cos his bum's up there, there's Wise 'cos he's down there," you could go along the line and work out who it was. Then we get a call from the FA and me and Bobby have to go to the FA to answer about the picture. "You must have been paid for this," they said. So we told them the story. "No, you must have got a reward," and they hit us with a £750 each fine. We got no win bonus for the cup so it actually cost us money. The start of the season me and Sanch would go in and talk about bonus schemes. Sam [Hammam] said, "You could put down £1m for winning the cup!" but then thought he better not put that just in case. We got appearance money, but no win bonus, but the lads that played in the Charity Shield, they got nice appearance money which was like a cup bonus.'

Beasant would leave the club that summer, bringing to an end his long reign between the sticks at Wimbledon, but he recalled what it was like to be part of the story. 'Dave Bassett was our mentor. He took us through the leagues, and I would say not just the player, but the man I am, is down to Bassett. He put a lot of good traits in me and the lads. If you were weak-minded, you wouldn't survive at Wimbledon. Very much a place for men to stand up and be counted, not just in a game but every day in training, and if you couldn't handle it you wouldn't last at the club. Ian Holloway, he's a bit of a character, a personality on TV. He came and he struggled, a west country boy who wasn't used to the banter we used to give him. We'd do shooting practice, and we had no nets, so when it went behind the goal in the stinging nettles he'd get the nickname Stinger, as he'd fetch the balls and say in his thick accent, "I'd best get that ball out them stingers!" He found it tough but when you see him now he must have learned a lot from it, but at the time he couldn't handle it.

'Bassett left. It was his second attempt at leaving. The first, we went up north to play a game, and after we got back and off at King's Cross, we'd go into Frank McLintock's pub there and have a few beers. He was his normal self and he finally told us, "I've made a decision, I'm going to Crystal Palace," and we had him up against the wall saying you aren't going anywhere. He went, but knew he'd made a mistake. But he made the move. He'd taken us from Division Four, and I was the same. My ambition was to play in the top flight and I'd never had dreamed it would be for the first club I signed for in the fourth. I thought if I want to play at the top, I'll have to leave the club. So Bassett said, "I've gone as far as I can go," and I'm thinking the same way.

'Don Howe was coming in and he's told me, "You're in our mind for England," but my thoughts are, "I'm in your mind, but I won't get picked while I'm playing for Wimbledon." We had a stigma; people didn't want Dons players playing for England. So I said that to Don, I wanted to go to a bigger club and he said, "You're not going, but I'll let you know if someone comes in for you. I promise." After we beat Newcastle in the cup run, Bobby said, "Newcastle have come in for you, £350,000." Blimey, that's a lot of money, but he said, "I told them to come back with £1m." I thought no one's ever going to pay that for a goalkeeper. And that was it. "I said I'd tell you but you're not going." So the cup run went on and after we won he turned to me and said, "I bet you're pleased I turned down that offer now." I got a call in the summer from Bob saying they made another offer and it's been accepted. "What's the fee then if you accepted it?" "That's not for me to tell you, so you need to speak to them." Newcastle rang me up and said come and chat, and that's how it happened.

'I'm so pleased I can say I played for Wimbledon, at Plough Lane, that was my home. I never had to ground-share, I never had to go through the stupidness of going to Milton Keynes, and if you're going to pick a game to go out on why not pick the biggest game in football history.'

The Fans' Memories

Terry Hunt

I was 15 years old and on that Saturday was doing my Duke of Edinburgh Bronze award walk. We started from Redhill and were heading for an overnight stop at Box Hill. The teachers told us no radios or Walkmans and speakers (google them if you're too young to know!). How was I to know what was going on in what was to become such a famous afternoon?

Of course, in my rucksack was said Walkman and a set of speakers. Attached to my rucksack was a scarf and a flag and once I was up on to Reigate Hill crossing the A217 before heading into the countryside, quite a few cars were honking their horns and some cheers were coming from car windows.

Once at Box Hill and with tents pitched, we were ready to go for the 3pm kick-off. A load of us huddled round my tent listening in anticipation of the final, me being the only Dons fan among us. I had never listened to a match on the radio before and I remember it being really weird not knowing who was cheering in the stadium and for what they were cheering.

All I do remember was when we scored and, once I realised we had scored, I jumped for joy and started running round my tent shouting and cheering. Wimbledon had taken the lead over Liverpool in the FA Cup Final. This was not in the script! And running around drawing the attention of your schoolteachers who had banned radios was not the best of ideas.

Then the penalty, head in hands, waiting, and back to more confusing cheers. Had Liverpool scored, had Beasant saved it? More running around the tent like a 15-year-old loon. This time though, the teachers did come over to see what all the fuss was about. Thinking the worst and trying to hide the radio and speakers, we fessed up and told the teachers what was going on. I think the look on my face as if to say 'please don't take it away, we're winning' allowed me to keep the radio on until the final whistle, and that seemed like an eternity.

And to the final whistle, more jumping around and even some mates who weren't Wimbledon fans started jumping around. History had been made and the Crazy Gang beat the Culture Club!

Radio off.

On a separate note, my chemistry teacher at the time was Stephen Crabtree. Every end of term after the win he would do a quiz. Q1 was always, 'Who won the FA Cup in 1988?' (I seem to remember every other question was the same one.)

Anyway, that is my memory of cup final day. I couldn't go although some family members did, but even so, it was a great way to listen to it and celebrate it!

Stephen Godfrey

I joined the army in 1975, so had not been able to attend many matches in the years leading up to the final. I had been posted to West Germany in 1984, so we didn't even have *Match of the Day* as best I can remember, let alone any coverage of lower-league football.

In May 1988, I had just started a tour in West Belfast. Despite all that was going on, I followed the Dons' progress closely. As the big day approached, I managed to stay back in barracks on admin duties, one of which was organising TVs for the troops. I arranged the spare tellies around the block, so I was never out of sight of one of the sets, so I could get on with my tasks without missing one moment of our great Wembley day.

At the final whistle, I leapt and whooped around the empty block like the crazy gangster I felt like. I spent the rest of the day trying to impress anyone who would listen that the mighty Dons had won the cup! None of them were interested. Probably why I have hated all Kentish teams since (I was serving with the Queen's Regiment, who recruited mostly in Kent).

John Martin

In the lead-up to the cup final the BBC showed highlights of Liverpool beating Nottingham Forest 5-0 in a league match a couple of weeks earlier. It must have been one of the most complete performances I have ever seen. Liverpool could have scored ten, and I was scared that the cup final was going to be embarrassingly one-sided. Me and my friends agreed on the way to the match that a 3-0 or 4-0 defeat would not be too embarrassing.

Apart from the goal and Beasant's penalty save (never a penalty after a fine tackle from Goodyear), both of which were up the end where I was standing, my main memory of the match was that there were thousands of Liverpool fans in our end. I guess there was 20–25,000 Wimbledon fans in the stadium, but the rest of the 98,000 seemed to be supporting Liverpool. Leaving the ground, my one memory is of walking down Wembley Way and seeing a group of Liverpool fans sitting on the pavement, heads in hands, saying, 'We wouldn't have minded losing to ANYONE apart from Wimbledon!' We consoled them …

A group of us had driven to the ground together and halfway back home we decided to go back via Wimbledon town centre 'just in case anyone was there celebrating'. With hindsight it seems crazy to think that we just popped into town on the off-chance, but that was how it was. Of course, we got halfway down Wimbledon Hill, and the traffic came to a halt. Nothing moved for a while, during which time another fan passed some beers into the car (we had Wimbledon flags on display).

After a while we decided to park up and walk into town. We finally managed to get a drink in the Alex and stood outside to take in the atmosphere. Two memories of the evening – firstly, a chap, beer in hand, three stories up a scaffolding-clad building on the High Street, hanging out over the road joining in the songs; and second, the sound of broken glass crunching beneath my feet as so many beer glasses had been smashed during the celebrations.

What a day!

Steve Dowse

I was a student in North Wales in 1988, so the only games I saw in the cup run were the third-round victory against West Brom, where Dennis Wise completely ran the show and I could see just what an incredible player he'd become, and the semi-final against Luton. I remember going to buy a ticket for the semi from Plough Lane, asking if any tickets were left for White Hart Lane, and being met with the slightly sarcastic response, 'Are there any tickets left? How many do you want?' The papers went on endlessly about how small the crowd was going to be and how we'd rattle around the ground. In the end, I think we may have outnumbered the Luton fans and there was a good atmosphere among the Dons faithful. By half-time, we'd been dominant, and I was convinced we'd rue missed chances, a feeling which only increased when Mick Harford gave the Hatters the lead. However, a Fash penalty (I swear I've never seen a shot roll more slowly into the goal) and a Wisey goal, where he met a Corky cross with both feet from a yard out, allayed our fears. We were on our way to Wembley.

A couple of weeks before the final, I watched Liverpool destroy Nottingham Forest on *Sportsnight*. The final score was 5-0 but they could have got ten. Tom Finney called it 'one of the finest exhibitions of football I've ever seen in my life'. Suddenly, I was rather nervous for our chances.

As I was a member of the supporters' club at the time, I was guaranteed a couple of tickets for the final. I gave my extra ticket to my girlfriend Ingrid (now my wife), who was about to go to her first-ever game. The big day arrived, and our family took the train to Wimbledon, not knowing what to expect but absolutely determined to enjoy our big day.

I remember arriving at Plough Lane and seeing all the old-fashioned Routemaster buses parked along Weir Road, waiting to take us all to the game. Eventually, dozens of buses and hundreds of fans set off, and I'm sure I wasn't alone in reading the morning newspapers on the way, where every journalist and 'expert' was predicting that, for the good of football, Liverpool would win by at least four or five goals. They predicted a massacre and wanted the noisy upstarts from SW19 to go back to non-league where they belonged. The team would have needed to do nothing more than pin those articles to the dressing room wall;

that would be all the motivation they'd need. And that's exactly what they did.

As our bus approached the twin towers, it was clear that the Dons would be heavily outnumbered by Liverpool fans; Wembley Way was a sea of red. I remember a Liverpool fan asking to 'swap' his ticket with me as I'd get a much better view from the Liverpool end, but even I wasn't that gullible. When it was finally time to go into the ground, I was struck by how run down and dilapidated Wembley was, a world away from the billion-pound arena that stands there today. Although we were up in the gods, we still had a pretty good view. With quite a lot of time to kill, there was an 'all-star' game before kick-off; it was quite strange to see David Frost and Rod Stewart representing the Dons (Rod seemed to particularly enjoy running up and down the wing), but I just wanted the main event to get going.

Finally, the game began. Perhaps because it all happened so long ago, my memories of the match are somewhat hazy. The first half seemed to pass by in a blur. Initially, Liverpool just seemed to keep possession without really doing much with it. Gradually, they began to impose themselves on the game; Dave Beasant brilliantly clawed the ball away from John Barnes, preventing a certain goal. Then, on 35 minutes, Peter Beardsley shrugged off a clumsy Andy Thorn challenge to score. However, referee Brian Hill had already blown his whistle for the foul and play was brought back for a free kick. Cue a collective sigh of relief among the Dons faithful, who were asking themselves why the ref hadn't used the advantage rule. I couldn't help feeling that a Liverpool goal was coming.

Perhaps not! Barely a minute or two later, a Steve Nicol foul led to a fantastic Dennis Wise free kick and that goal. Lawrie Sanchez leapt up to glance the ball into the net. After a split second of disbelief, there was pandemonium on the terraces. I just remember hugging Ingrid and jumping up and down. One-nil at half-time. We'd more than held our own, but could we really hang on?

To be honest, I remember even less about the second half. Liverpool would hold keep of the ball, move it forward and we would clear it. The Dons threw themselves at every shot and defended heroically. Then on the hour, a through ball went towards John Aldridge, who was running into the area. Clive Goodyear slid in brilliantly and played the ball cleanly. Even from high in the terrace, I could see what an excellent tackle it was, and so could every Dons fan around me. Perhaps to make up for his earlier error, the ref gave a penalty. Aldridge had not missed a penalty that season, but his body language suggested that the pressure might have got to him. Big Dave dived low to his left and history was made. Joy and pandemonium again. Ingrid said how sorry she felt for Aldridge; I couldn't care less.

As the game wore on, Liverpool attacks and Wimbledon defending became more and more desperate but, apart from one near miss from Craig Johnston right at the end, I felt more and more confident that we'd hold on. On the final whistle, I couldn't help thinking about how far the club had come since I first watched them in the Southern League. We'd taken on the league champions, beaten them and now Dave was going up to lift the FA Cup. What a way to stick two fingers up at the writers who had condemned us to defeat in the papers that morning. Seeing Dave (who was definitely the man of the match) raise the trophy aloft was a moment that I regularly think about to this day.

On the bus home, there seemed to be a stunned silence. It had been a long and emotional day and I think there may have been a sense of disbelief for our achievement. Perhaps it only began to sink in when we arrived back in Wimbledon, and we saw crowds of people celebrating. However, we decided to go back to my mum and dad's; there was no way we were going to get a beer that evening! There were even more people in Wimbledon town centre the following day and it was impossible to see very much. My parents managed to get into the civic reception, where my mum collected autographs. She said Vinnie Jones was 'lovely but hungover'. There were more than a few sore heads that day; the victory had captured the town's imagination like never before.

I can't believe it was 35 years ago.

Jerzy Dabrowski

Mansfield away. I think I remember more of the fan interactions and trouble rather than the game itself. On paper I didn't think the game would attract a lot of interest. Not sure how much Wimbledon were seen as a giant-killing scalp, despite the difference in divisions of the two sides. I seem to remember part of the ground being closed off, probably as a result of the concerns following the Bradford fire and a larger-than-expected home and away turnout. This resulted in loads of people outside just before the game. With the away end very crowded some of us were filtered into the Mansfield end, with police trying to separate us inside. I remember a terribly wet and muddy pitch, a rare goal from Terry Phelan and a penalty save by Dave Beasant. Then it was back to dodging bottles, rocks and fists on the way back to the car!

Watford at home; I don't remember much from this game. Malcolm Allen playing up the whole game, and deservedly getting the reaction it merited. Playing with ten men but still being the better side and elbowing my mate's girlfriend in the head when we scored our winner. I think that was her first and last Wimbledon game, but they did get married!

Luton Town in the semi-final; my main memory of this fixture was the draw for the semi-final. Live on BBC Radio if I recall correctly, Monday lunchtime, I sat with two other Wimbledon fans hoping to avoid Nottingham

Forest and Liverpool. When they were drawn out the cheer was probably as loud as when we won the game.

Somehow I managed to get a spare ticket for this game, so dragged my Scottish flatmate to his first football match. A game we should have won in the first half; I could not believe it when Mick Harford put them a goal up. But being Wimbledon I knew this meant nothing. Dennis Wise with probably his worst ever finish to win the game, and the calmest penalty you will ever see in an FA Cup semi-final. I think I was in so much disbelief at getting to the FA Cup Final I went home after a couple of celebratory beers to let it sink in.

For Wembley, it was definitely the earliest I had woken up for a game in London. I bought some beers for the car journey but not too many – if we somehow won the cup I wanted to remember it! For a bizarre reason, our 'designated driver' to away games thought it would be a good idea to go by car for this one. I did think that this was going to be my one regret as I always envisaged going to a cup final on a packed tube train and then walking up Wembley Way. But car it was, and Wembley Way was missed as we parked right by it instead.

On the plus side, it meant for a memorable journey home. It was a beautiful, hot, sunny day so the car windows were all wound down, with scarves hanging out, ribbons attached flowing in the breeze. People in the street and other cars shouted, cheered, and signalled their congratulations all the way back to Wimbledon. The highlight was the final stretch into Wimbledon Village. As we approached the Dog and Fox pub, one of the patrons sitting outside ran across the road to our car, held up by the traffic. One full, cold pint was thrust into my hand as he congratulated us and said, 'You deserve this!'

And so it was for the rest of the evening. Down in Wimbledon the streets had hundreds of fans spilling into them, the pubs emptying as they ran out of beer.

The game?! Well, everyone knows what happened, but it wasn't that enjoyable as Liverpool looked so dangerous. But we had some luck; Beardsley's goal should not have been disallowed. We deserved it, as most of the Liverpool fans told us when we finally left the ground. So stunned were some of us, they even told us, 'Cheer up! You won the bloody thing!'

Chris Prodromou (Liverpool fan)

I remember Wimbledon doing a thing if you went to the last three home games of the season you could get tickets for the final and I know a lot of Liverpool fans that did that. I actually backed Wimbledon to win the cup at 33/1 at the third-round stage. I won money but was still gutted we lost. It was a lovely warm day from what I remember, all good-natured fun before and after the game. No trouble except with some Chelsea fans who turned up, but the Dons fans were boss.

Mark Leadon

Rather than just the Wembley final, my recollections are more based around the whole of that season. As we kicked off in August, I am sure many Dons fans were apprehensive and feared the worst. Not only did we face the dreaded 'second season syndrome' but it was going to be without some of our star names. Nigel Winterburn, arguably the best ever Wimbledon player, had been snapped up on the cheap by Arsenal while homegrown talent such as Mark Morris and more worryingly Glyn Hodges had secured better pay deals elsewhere. The worst news, of course, was that Dave 'Harry' Bassett, our long-ball guru who had guided us from the depths of the Fourth Division, had exited and was teaming up with Elton John at Watford. Even with the news of Bobby Gould taking over along with experienced Don Howe as his number two, I am sure many of us thought that this could signal the white flag being hoisted and a spiral back down the leagues from whence we came.

Gould, to his credit, was astute. Rather than tinkering with the system which had proved so successful, he continued with it. If it doesn't need fixing then why try and mend it? Long ball was still in and Fash, Wise, Beasant, Jones, Thorne, Sanchez et al were left to continue to 'hit those corner flags', compete for 'second balls', pump the box with crosses and play it long rather than through the midfield. I, for one, breathed a huge sigh of relief at this news.

While the league was more than comfortable, finishing seventh, just one place behind the memorable inaugural top-flight season, it was in the FA Cup where the real excitement took place. Although I didn't go away at St James' Park, the news that we won in this fifth-round tie after all the hype regarding 'Vinnie v Gazza round two' started to get you to believe.

A home draw would do nicely in the quarters and the footballing gods were kind. Home to Watford with the prodigal sons of Hodges and Mark Morris returning, albeit without the already sacked Bassett. The first half was a disaster; a goal down and Brian Gayle sent off. At half-time I'm sure most of us would have settled for a draw and taking them back to Vicarage Road. This team were no shrinking violets though. After experiencing defeat in last year's FA Cup at the same stage, they simply were not going to let this happen again. Gould and Howe came up trumps at the break, sacrificing forward Alan Cork and putting on Eric Young at centre-back to fill the void after the red card. Young indeed got the equaliser while Fashanu slotted home the winner in front of an ecstatic West Bank.

The draw for the semis was kind with us avoiding the big guns of Liverpool and Nottingham Forest and pairing us with Luton. A short trip to White Hart Lane was the venue which I remember also being happy with. Before the match, I had no doubt in my mind that this was going to be our game. Walking down the endless Seven Sisters

Road to the ground was, as always, an athletic event, but I remember being pleased to see more Dons fans than I expected. Once we got inside the stadium, yes, we were in a minority, but this was not the usual massive fan imbalance and this again gave me optimism.

Wimbledon hammered the Hatters and should have been three or four up before Mick Hartford undeservedly tucked away a through ball. However, again the metaphoric sleeves were rolled up; we were never going to lose. Thankfully Andy Dibble, their keeper who had kept them in the game first half, turned from hero to villain, dropping a cross and bringing down Gibson for a penalty. Oh the pressure on Fashanu but he slowly rolled the ball to the keeper's left as 'Officer Dibble' dived to his right. Standing on the Shelf I could hardly watch but thankfully Fash kept his nerve. After the equaliser, there was only going to be one winner. Cork hooked over a cross and Wisey made no mistake by sliding in seemingly with two feet at the far post. Not without a scare or two, but we held on; Wimbledon were in the FA Cup Final!

During the build-up for the final, we were on the TV a lot. Players buying their suits I think was one programme, interviews with some of our players on another. Pundits gave us no chance with some predicting a hatful of goals for the champions. But for me I never thought we were completely out of it. Our league record in the two years against Liverpool, which included a Corky headed winner at Anfield, meant that we undoubtedly had a fighter's chance. There was no doubt we were ready for a scrap too.

By this time I had moved away from my south London and Battersea roots. I now lived in Watford and taught in a local secondary school. What I didn't know was that northern football fans used Watford as a stop-off point. They drove down, parked their cars in the town's car parks and travelled the last few miles by train from Watford Junction station. So there I am in my yellow and blue scarf next to hundreds of Scousers in the carriage. 'Hey lad, how many will you let in today?' 'Five, six or seven?' 'Aldridge or Barnes hat-trick do you reckon?' It was constant. All good-natured but something I could have done without.

At the ground, it was a similar situation. Outnumbered everywhere. I had a spare ticket and am still proud of myself that despite countless Reds asking to buy any ticket for an inflated price, I sold it to a Dons fan who needed one at face value. Once in the ground there was something immediately obviously wrong with the ticketing allocation. Whole sections down our end had Liverpool fans in. There's no doubt that the club, probably under Hammam's guidance, gave sections of our tickets to the opposition. If this is correct, an unforgivable misguided decision.

As for the game itself, we held them quite comfortably. I know Liverpool's 'beef' regarding their disallowed goal because the ref blew up too early. However, you heard the whistle even from the stands loud and clear and I am convinced Beasant never really committed to the save knowing it wouldn't be given anyway. Our goal was classic Wimbledon – we had seen it many times before. Free kick delivered expertly by Dennis Wise with Lawrie Sanchez glancing it in. We had a fantastic view from behind the goal and I am so glad we scored it attacking our fans.

Could we hang on? The second half dragged but to be honest it was still reasonably comfortable. Until that penalty. Never in a million years was that a foul. Goodyear clearly got the ball. Everyone knew it apart from Hill the ref. It was a shocker! Thank God, Lurch did his homework and clawed it away to earn himself legendary status. As the game closed out, the nerves increased. One thing strangely I recall. I turned to my mate. 'How long's left?' 'Five,' he replied. Well five minutes later I asked again, 'How long's left?' 'Still four,' he cried! Time literally stood still, and it was the longest last few minutes I can ever recall. Hold out we did though, and the rest is history!

After the game, I have a few recollections. During the latter half of the season the popular chant from the West Bank was, 'When Dave goes up to lift the FA Cup, we'll be there, we'll be there.' As we went down the steps to exit after the presentation and parading of the cup, the cry had changed to the past tense. Loud and clear from our fans was the new version, 'When Dave went up to lift the FA Cup, we were there, we were there.' It dawned on me that I had just witnessed sporting history. I also remember walking past a stalwart Dons fan. He still watches AFC Wimbledon now. He was sitting on a Wembley step crying his eyes out. This is what football does for people and it was just so emotional.

On the way home, I had to get on that train back to Watford Junction with all those Liverpool fans. Should I take off my lucky scarf, I wondered? Was it going to antagonise them? Well I didn't and to be fair to them, not one caused me any grief and a couple even shook my hand and said, 'Well done, you deserved it.' One said, 'I'll see you at the Charity Shield!' My thoughts on the train were not reliving the game but actually about where we came from. 'Little Wimbledon' who I had seen, sitting in the south stand as a young boy with my grandad, dad and brother in the Southern League, had somehow won the oldest cup competition in the world. Fairy tales can come true!

Mark Sheppard

Yes, I was there, it wasn't just about the match but being in Wimbledon town centre before going to Wembley. Then after the match how crazy it was back in Wimbledon. One memory for me was meeting my friends in the Alex before the match. One of my friends brought her spaniel and she had tied a Dons scarf to him. Outside the Alex kids petted him and he was very friendly. When taken into the bar he spotted another dog and reared up, growling. Dons fans at the bar turned to Robin and chanted 'psycho, psycho' to him. This was the chant that the West Bank used to salute Vinnie Jones. The dog was very proud of himself, and that scarf seemed to embolden him.

The other thing I remember was how crazy Wimbledon was after the match. One guy was standing on top of a bus as it came into the Broadway from Worple Road. They shut the road eventually. The Village was just as crazy. You couldn't get a drink because there were no glasses left. One thing I remember from the match was that penalty and this little Scouser who had been in our end came running upstairs from the loo or bar or somewhere. He made it just in time to see Aldridge screw it up and big Dave making history. That day we reached a summit and while we had many seasons in the top flight we never reached those heights again. Probably at that point we needed serious investment, but it never came.

Paul Cade

My cup final memory is Fash on the edge of the box leaping up in the air when the penalty was saved, and it was never shown on any of the TV coverage. So for that reason I have always treasured that silly memory.

Jamie Porter

My parents split up when I was a really young child and I lived with my mum and my two older brothers in Gloucestershire. Dad lived in Clapham and when spending weekends with him we would go and watch either Chelsea or Wimbledon, whoever was at home really. Dad had a big soft spot for us even though he grew up a Leicester fan; his best and oldest friend from Mitcham Grammar is a lifelong Womble. As an impressionable seven-year-old, the cup final in 1988 cemented that Wimbledon was the club for me. I watched the game on TV with my brothers in our house near Stroud and spent the remainder of the afternoon until darkness fell attempting to recreate the free kick from Dennis Wise and header from Lawrie Sanchez, with my middle brother the goalkeeper, attempting Dave Beasant-like heroics between our jumper goalposts.

I wasn't at the game. I have been a sporadic matchday attendee due to living all over the UK and now Australia, so no one will know me from the Wimbledon community (with the exception of Dad's old mate) but I hope this puts a smile on someone's face.

Matthew Hunt

My memories of '88 are slightly different as I didn't go to the game. I was a 15-year-old living in Norwich. I was unable to get a ticket so watched it at home with my Wimbledon-supporting dad who used to sell programmes at Plough Lane in the '60s as a young lad. At that time, I was ridiculed for supporting the Dons, which made me love them even more. I was so confident that we would win that I took on every bet thrown my way that Liverpool would win.

I made a note of them all in my homework diary; this included teachers too, nobody gave us a chance. Mars bars were the allowed betting currency at the time, and I racked up 48 individual bets. Obviously, Wimbledon won, and I collected my dues. I didn't eat a single Mars until I had them all and sat in my room scooping them up in my arms like gold coins. Marvellous times.

Matt Crompton

I was at Bradford University from 1986 to '89. One of my best mates I met there was a Liverpool fan. I stood in the Kop with two other mates when we won [at Anfield] in 1987. As a member of the Wimbledon Independent Supporters' Association I got two tickets. My girlfriend at the time had no interest in football so I took Pete, a Blackburn Rovers fan, with me. I was a pinprick of yellow and blue in a sea of red and white on the M1. It was all a rush to get there up on the tube.

In the ground I was in a side section near the halfway line with quite a few Liverpool in our section. Enjoyed the Frost Dons v Tarbuck Reds. We were lucky with that disallowed goal, and then watching Wise line up that free kick, unbelievable scenes as that went in. Then throughout the second half both of us thought Liverpool were crap, not creating many real chances. I remember another Don saying, 'Take this in because this is a once-in-a-lifetime moment.' He was so right. Then taking in the celebrations after the cup was lifted by Beasant. Then back to Bradford, I should have stayed in Putney with my dad and gone to the testimonial, that's my only regret. The big change is the lack of drinking I did then compared with 2016 before that play-off final. An amazing day!

Anthony Sirkett

My best memory of the cup final is after the game. Me and three mates, Dean Gould, Darren Campbell and Ian Cameron, in Putney High Street and we spotted the team coach coming through. Waving our flags, Bobby Gould sitting at the front with the cup in his lap, saw us and gave us our own personal trophy lift! What a moment!

Ted Finch

I am sure there are plenty of AFC Wimbledon supporters who, like me, saw every round up to and including Wembley. However, my personal memory comes from the day after the final. Having watched the cup raised at the Town Hall, I retired with a friend to the Alexandra, to 'toast the Dons' success'. While there we were engaged in conversation by an attractive young lady. Lulu and I have now been married for over 31 years.

Mike Clement

My brother Andy was in the squad, and we went back to the team hotel. We had my grandmother on the phone and

Dave Beasant walked past and we got him to chat to her. She didn't believe it was him. Great day.

Graham Cooksley

Our attendance at the 1988 FA Cup Final has its origins in the 1984 FA Cup semi-final between Plymouth Argyle and Watford. Being born and bred in Plymouth and supporting Argyle, a family friend who had a relation who worked for the Football League secured our tickets in the North Stand at Villa Park for my 15-year-old self and my dad.

As is usual the invitation was always, 'Well if you fancy cup final tickets anytime just let me know.' Argyle lost that semi-final so requesting tickets for the '84 final was never on the agenda and of course actions speak louder than words and the 1985, '86 and '87 finals all came and went with enquires for tickets coming to nothing. All that changed in 1988 when around the quarter-final stage we politely asked again and just after the semi-finals news came back that we are able to get two seated tickets for the Wimbledon v Liverpool final.

The seats themselves cost £17.50 on the lower tier just to the left-hand side of the Royal Box when in the stadium, which allowed us a good view of Princess Di taking to the pitch to meet the teams after the long walk from the old players' tunnel. I recall the seats were in the Liverpool 'end' of Wembley although that did not stop my dad supporting Wimbledon for the day mainly because he had met someone he knew through his trade union connections before the match outside the stadium and this chap happened to be a Wimbledon fan, while I might have verged on supporting Liverpool mainly because that team of Aldridge, Barnes and Beardsley had played some great football that season.

Part of the thrill of the old Wembley was the buzz of the gathering crowds outside the stadium and the grimness of the concourses under the stands and of course the infamous toilets. In contrast the first glimpse of the pitch and the bowl of the stadium took the breath away and then seeing the place slowly fill up with the empty standing terraces slowly becoming a sea of banners and scarfs while the blue and red seats were slowly replaced by people bedecked in their team's colours all given a voice by the noise generated and enhanced by the stadium's enclosing roof. Strangely in real life Wembley seemed smaller than the TV version of the stadium.

As to the match itself, it all seemed to be played out in double quick time in the stadium. I recall impressive comments from those sat around us when I mentioned about Beasant's penalty save being the first in an FA Cup Final and the expectation from the Liverpool fans every time they got the ball near the Wimbledon goal, they would score, that team always scored. Of course they didn't score and at the end of the game those around us emptied out fairly quick while all the celebrations took place at the other end of the stadium. For two neutrals it did not really matter either way and eventually we left the stadium and into the endless traffic jams which went hand-in-hand with getting away from the Wembley car parks and lead at some point to the M4 and the south-west.

Mike Dowek

I had been following the Dons since December 1974, so I had witnessed the incredible, almost surreal rise from Southern League to the First Division. In the run-up to the 1988 final a small group of friends and I had followed our full cup run, including memorable trips to Mansfield and Newcastle. The atmosphere at Newcastle was particularly hostile and I remember all the Dons fans being herded back to the train station after the game fully surrounded by a Roman square formation of police officers to safeguard our escape. The real pressure match in that cup run was the semi-final versus Luton at White Hart Lane. We just desperately wanted to get to Wembley, so when we saw Fash's penalty trickle over the line to equalise, followed by Wisey's winner, the relief was immense. We were on our way!

Having such a small fanbase with almost half of Wembley to fill, tickets for the final proved very easy to come by for Wimbledon fans. We were able to get tickets for a wider group of friends who were normally supporters of other clubs, Palace, Chelsea and West Ham among others, but were happy to be 'Dons for the day'. Among that group was my recently acquired girlfriend (now my wife of 30-plus years), Jane, who considered herself a Chelsea fan, but was actually not that into football and just wanted to experience the occasion.

The day came and we all travelled up to Wembley. Our group all had tickets for the standing area behind the goal and I carried Jane's and my ticket in the inside pocket of my jacket. It was a raucous and chaotic atmosphere outside the stadium and unsurprisingly we were massively outnumbered by Liverpool fans, many of whom had turned up without tickets. Many others had managed to acquire tickets for the Wimbledon end. As we were approaching the stadium, I took out our tickets to check which entrance we were meant to use, then put them back. After this my friend David did the same, but before he could put it away again, a passing Liverpool fan snatched it out of his hand. I saw this and managed to snatch it back and return it to David. I was then bundled over by a small group of Liverpool fans but after a few seconds they left me alone and ran off. I then realised that they had stolen the two tickets out of my inside pocket which they must have seen me take out before.

I tried to report the theft to the police but frankly they weren't very interested. In any case I wouldn't have been able to identify the culprits and, given that they had taken unallocated standing tickets, there would have been no way to trace them in the stadium among hundreds of other Liverpool fans who had infiltrated the Wimbledon end.

So that was it, Jane and I were going to have to miss the cup final, the highlight of my footballing life thus far. I was completely heartbroken. That is until another one of my friends, Carolyn (a West Ham fan, married to a Palace supporter) stepped up. She very kindly insisted that I take her ticket, then she and Jane would go back and watch on TV (there was still just enough time left for them to do this). So I got to see the game after all.

Needless to say our expectations for the match itself were pretty low. We were obviously massive underdogs and Liverpool were league champions and possibly the best club side in the world at that time. What happened next is of course well documented, Wise free kick, Sanchez header, Aldridge penalty, Beasant save, Crazy Gang/Culture Club, Princess Di. We only went and won the bloody cup! I remember after the game, as we were leaving the stadium, we were all in a state of wonderment and disbelief. Some (kinder) Liverpool fans approached us afterwards to congratulate us and, seeing the bemused shock on our faces, said, 'Cheer up, you won!'

We returned home, reunited with Jane and Carolyn, and of course all headed to the pub to get very, very drunk. On the day of the open-top bus parade we joined the joyful throng in Wimbledon town centre. A massive crowd, it seemed like the whole town had turned up to celebrate this great moment of civic pride. After over 34 years, while I don't think I have ever fully got over the upsetting events before the match, my main memories are still filled with elation, pride – and disbelief.

Simon Wright (West Bromwich Albion fan)

Another season, another early exit.

For a club who had over a century's worth of experience in the FA Cup, WBA's cup record in the mid-1980s was dismal. Their last cup victory was four years previously in a scrambled 1-0 replay with Scunthorpe. The Baggies were a struggling Second Division club, whose primary ambition was to stay out of the third tier. The ball jiggling in blue bag outcome in early 1988 produced only a fatalistic reaction from supporters. 'Wimbledon away – fifth in the First Division? No chance!'

There were plus points. A new ground – the Baggies had never previously played Wimbledon. A London match was popular with supporters and players alike for an overnighter while the London Baggies were both numerous and well organised. And it's the FA Cup, it remains special for fans of a club with such an impressive track record overall. This made little sense; the previous season, fourth-tier Swansea City had easily defeated the Baggies, just the latest early exit among several. And yet interest in the fixture was much higher than for most league games resulting in an impressively large following, cynical though they were and very unimpressed with Plough Lane. 'It's a dog hole' was one of the less colourful phrases heard in the away end.

First Division prices were a shock to some, and I vividly remember an exchange with one Wimbledon programme seller. 'No, I just want to buy a programme, not the whole club.'

The Baggies fielded the usual mix of cynical pros, cheap veterans and a few up and going [sic] talent. The latter group included a wobbly Don Goodman, a raw and ill-disciplined Carlton Palmer and a youthful David Burrows. All were to be later sold and would build their reputations elsewhere. The antique main striker – as in terms of knowing how to score – Andy Gray couldn't play and alarmingly neither could West Brom's senior goalkeeper. Rookie keeper David Powell was called upon. He was soon to retire at the age of 21 for a new career selling fertiliser.

On a very windy day, Albion attacked from the start, subduing the Dons and creating the best chances while looking the better side for 40 minutes. Defender Stacey North's in-swinging cross was tipped over by 'Lurch' and then he headed into the net only for the goal to be disallowed for some obscure reason. Even so, the Baggies' Scottish striker Bobby Williamson missed the best chance. He had only Beasant to beat but screwed his shot hopelessly wide. ('The easiest opening of all,' lamented Ron Atkinson post-match.) His striking partner Goodman was put clear only to be hauled to the ground by Andy Thorn, who was lucky to escape with a caution. As the *Birmingham Sports Argus* said, 'Albion had the Dons in all sorts of undignified trouble.' Even Albion's George 'Rambo' (the title was ironic) Reilly got involved, heading just over from a corner.

The rot set in when the Baggies' five-man defence allowed Fashanu to score with a free header just before the break. Nobody picked up the cross from Wise once he dodged clear of Hopkins. Cue familiar discordant wailing in the away end of 'here we go again'. There was little that could be done about Wise's superb 30-yard shot for the second goal on 54 minutes. Williamson got there as quick as he could and the Scot was booked for his late lunge on Wise, who needed attention for four minutes and was later substituted.

The second half was a familiar Albion let-down. Beasant made full use of the wind at his back by regularly taking shots, aided by a linesman who seemed to think 1988 was the Be Kind to Offside Forwards Year, and a disappearing Albion defence. Abysmal marking led to two more Wimbledon goals while precisely no one was consoled by the Williamson/Thorn own goal token score for the visitors. Manager Atkinson had clearly given up, leaving both his substitutes on the bench. The final scoreline flattered the home side yet was sufficient to become West Brom's worst FA Cup defeat for 21 years.

Jon Quinnell

I did a banner but never got to display it (a bedsheet I believe): 'Reds got loads of money, Reds'll spend the cash, Reds need loads of runny, 'Cos we got Fash the Bash'.

James Willis

This was the first season I started going to Plough Lane. The first match I went to was in November, a 2-0 win against Southampton (Cork and Fash I think). I went with my dad who was a Palace fan. He wouldn't take me to the semi-final but promised he would if we got to the final. I was 15 and I didn't know the score of the Luton game until full time and I remember running downstairs bouncing when I saw the result. We went up in one of the London buses from Plough Lane. We were surrounded by Scousers and were in the corner where Wise took the free kick. The biggest thing I can remember is the buses returning through the Wimbledon Village and the buses stopping, opening the doors and people piling on and celebrating. I went to the Town Hall the next day but the most fun was the testimonial the week after with the 21-bum salute. They were a fantastic team, and it was just a great season.

Daniel Huckfield

For me, the game was a bit of a blur but two memories stand out. Firstly hugging my dad at the end. He is a compulsive gambler and had only stopped gambling a couple of years before and Wimbledon was our 'thing', and it was a truly special moment. The other memory was having my Wimbledon flag nicked by a pissed-up reveller in the Village! What an amazing day and time in my life.

Barbara Byng

I met members of the team in the Fox and Grapes the night before the final. Spoke with Vinnie, who was advising us to get there early to make sure our small children were safe. It was very civilised. I seem to recall Fash having a couple of girls on his arm! They gravitated to me because I had a Dons cap on. No one else recognised them. It isn't a football pub.

Paul Gray

I remember walking to Wembley having parked some way away. Liverpool supporters everywhere, many without tickets. A polite Scouser asked if had a spare, I had one, showed him it and I then got swarmed on by a bunch of Reds. They all had tickets and said mine was fake. They showed me their 'genuine' tickets. Poor lads, all had fakes. Match was a blur for me, too nervous.

Iain Slater

We scored a goal, and they didn't. I remembered meeting some reasonably well-behaved Liverpool supporters before the game, only thing was they were wearing 'Double-Double winners' hats. Maybe one day. Sound of mournful violins. Then after the match lots of lorries to be seen going past the Alex with supporters stood on the cab.

Nick Douse

It was my second Wimbledon match. My first was the 4-1 win v West Brom in the same cup run. I went with my dad and cousin, wearing a Wimbledon rosette. Liverpool fans everywhere, asking who was going to win. I said Wimbledon. The crush outside the ground was pretty scary for ten-year-old me. Liverpool fans were great, when they saw me and my cousin, they created space for us in the crush shouting 'get back, there are kids here'. That made me forever convinced they are great fans and that any anti-Liverpool supporter narratives after Hillsborough were untrue. I only really remember the penalty save. I was right about the result though.

Jason Barrett

You may not have heard my story before, but in case you haven't then I stake my claim of one of the best stories without even being there. I was a Liverpool fan until just before my 16th birthday which was early 1985. Being young and living in Iver near Uxbridge, plus not having any family who were strong supporters of any particular club, I just like many others followed Liverpool as they were simply the best in my early years. It wasn't until my early teenage years that I found out that my dad's half-nephew played for West Ham and that my grandad's close friend was John Bond [the long-time West Ham player and manager of numerous clubs]. I only eventually found out when I asked how he managed to give me signed LFC footballs.

Peter Knowlson

It took my ten-year-old son from Dartford to Wembley on my Honda 90 (times wos 'ard). As we left, after the best sport-based day of my life, I was more than a little concerned what effect our Dons shirts and scarves would have on those 'hooligan Scousers'. I needn't have worried – Liverpool supporters, of all ages, just kept congratulating us. That certainly didn't follow the media narrative. Mind you, I'll never forgive them for effectively keeping us out of Europe.

Mark Cox

Mansfield away was the hardest game of the run. Sell-out crowd, edgy atmosphere and Mansfield missed a penalty late on.

Richard Crabtree

Mansfield was epic. Got there quite early – about 2pm – and as we got there the home turnstiles were shut so there was a big scramble to get down the other uncovered end. There was a bit of tape between the home and away fans. As virtually all the local clubs had been knocked out a load of nutters turned up looking for trouble. If Mansfield had scored their penalty, they would have gone on to win as the place was going mental but luckily 'Lurch' saved it and it knocked the stuffing out of them. Also Fash was virtually chopped in half by a Mansfield defender, possibly the most blatant penalty ever and the ref refused to give it.

At Newcastle there was a black lady in the seats wearing a prominent Wimbledon scarf. She got some terrible abuse from the home fans, and I was too cowardly to stand up for her.

Also at the end of the game a copper tried to stop me melting into the crowd, but I ignored him as I knew we would be a target for abuse. Also the police at the station were refusing admission to anyone without a rail ticket as Newcastle fans were looking for trouble. I was buzzing for days after that match due to the sheer brilliance of our performance.

Cane Fortunato

A mere 13-year-old, I missed the semi-final at White Hart Lane against Luton as I was playing out in Holland. The whole FA Cup day was recorded on VHS. My best memory seeing us beat Liverpool. I got a ball signed by the FA Cup-winning team and have a signed pic from Dave Beasant of him saving John Aldridge's penalty. I still have the road to Wembley flag which has slightly faded. I also remember that we had a spare ticket and we sold it for face value for £17. I've got the FA Cup single still kicking about somewhere.

Ian Dear

Me and my brother were on the train nearing Wembley and some Liverpool fans got on and because they went to Wembley every season they more or less said to us, 'Come on, boys, we will show you the way to the stadium,' so I said, 'That's OK, we will take the trophy back.'

Phil Russ

Me and a friend of a friend got the tube back home after the final. We got in a carriage rammed with Liverpool supporters and one fan said we should have been shouting and cheering as we had won!

Jan Letchford

I discharged myself from an Edinburgh hospital on Thursday having had knee surgery. I had to travel by coach to London on Friday to get to White Hart Lane on Saturday for the semi-final against Luton which was a nightmare as the hospital refused to give me crutches as I should not have been leaving, and I had to hobble. My dad drove me there. He wasn't allowed to drop me at the gates; the police said that because we didn't have a disabled badge we couldn't drop off, so he dropped me round the corner, and I hopped back while he parked the van. He then helped me to my seat. I saw the game and was very happy, in pain but happy. But I made the rookie mistake of wearing rope-soled espadrilles to Wembley. I'd never been before. Walking through those tunnels they soaked up all the piddle. I had wee-soaked feet the entire match, delightful, but walking home I didn't care, I was walking in the air!

Denis Garvey

The only game I missed was the semi-final v Luton as I was on a beach in Tunisia. Couldn't get any info on first half. Had to wait until 4.10pm to be able to tune into BBC World Service for commentary. Tense but worth every minute.

Steve Leahy

Aged 13 and getting on one of (it seemed!) 500 red London buses from Plough Lane was incredible. I remember singing the 'Dave goes up to lift the FA Cup' song all the way there.

The split second Sanch's 'glarrrrncing' header goes in, then when Lurch saved the penalty, it was pandemonium, and I remember hugging an old guy next to me. He was in floods of tears.

Arriving back at Plough Lane was great. Seeing the TV cameras and the thousands in yellow and blue outside. The following day outside the Town Hall was also a huge day.

Ray Armfield

The excitement really started after we beat Watford in the quarter-final. With Luton Town, Nottingham Forest and

Liverpool joining us in the semi-finals, there was no doubt who I wanted us to be paired with and I guess Hatters fans felt the same way about us. I was working in Southwark Crown Court on the day the semi-final draw was made, and a friendly usher said he would let me know the draw. When he caught my eye and mouthed the word 'Luton' I could barely suppress a reaction and it was enough to get me a quizzical look from the judge.

Once we'd got past Luton and made it to the final there was the inevitable worry about getting tickets, but I needn't have worried. Two season tickets and one club membership meant that I got my full allocation of ten and I ensured they went to people who would appreciate them, including a couple of lapsed Dons I hadn't seen since we were teenagers. I went to my local newsagents on the morning of the final and bought a copy of every daily newspaper and ordered another set for the following day. These were moments to be treasured and I wanted some mementos.

The one memento I didn't want (at the time), however, was being sold from a hastily erected trestle table on Wembley Way. We came out of the tube station to a sea of red with the occasional splash of yellow and blue and I noticed this lad selling t-shirts. 'Liverpool FC 1988 Double Winners', they proclaimed. This was BEFORE the match, remember. Everyone has their own memories of the match itself. But it flew by for me. At the end we hung around on the terrace to savour the moment and I met one of the friends I'd got a ticket for. 'Beats Hillingdon Borough away, doesn't it?' he said. And we both laughed. When we walked back up Wembley Way, I began looking in every rubbish bin. When my wife asked me why, I said, 'I want one of those Liverpool Double Winners shirts,' but I couldn't find one!

The following morning, I was up bright and early and looked forward to my stroll to the newsagents. It was so early the paperboys were still loading up their satchels. I gave a cheery 'good morning' to the one in the Liverpool shirt. He was first out of the door. Then, in a Mr Benn moment, the shopkeeper appeared. 'Ah, Mr Wimbledon! I have something for you. One of everything!' It was every newspaper that I'd ordered the previous day. I kept them for years before deciding to share them and they went for a sizeable sum in one of the AFC Wimbledon silent auctions I ran. Looking back now, the post-Wembley euphoria must have lasted a bit longer than I thought as our son was born ten months later!

Terence May

In the week leading up to the final my wife and I helped man the telephones in the club office during the evenings. You can imagine the pressure on the full-time day staff, so a break in the evenings was welcomed. On the Tuesday a chap came into the office, begging for a ticket and saying how he'd been a long-time supporter but somehow had missed out on buying one. After being told several times all had been sold someone at the reception desk told him if he could name the 1963 Amateur Cup-winning team then a ticket might be found. The fellow started but was asked to stop until I came from the back to check (I have followed the Dons since 1961). He started, Mick Kelly, Eddie Reynolds, Roy Law, err, ah, Eddie Reynolds. At this point I reminded him he had already said Eddie and asked if he wanted to start over. He did but after several silent minutes got as far as the same three players. At this point I ran through all 11 and he, looking crestfallen, looked across to the staff and said, 'I think I'd better go?' To the chorus of 'yes', he left.

Answering the phones on the Friday evening was most eventful with one of my first calls being from Floella Benjamin. She was very pleasant and wanted to know if her bouquet had arrived. To which I was able to reassure her that it had indeed and was on its way up to John Fashanu, the intended recipient. There followed a fairly long and warm chat before she hung up after wishing the club well.

Soon afterwards, the accent told me I had a Liverpool follower on the line. He, very politely, asked if there were any tickets left but after hearing me say, 'No, sorry,' he went into a tirade of how they couldn't have all been sold as 'your ****** tinpot club hasn't that many ******* supporters, and youse, you're ******* stupid'. Before putting the phone down on him, he was told, politely, 'I may be stupid, but I have a ticket.'

The best of all came just before we closed for the evening, and it was from a lovely, sweet, if maybe slightly eccentric elderly lady from Cheltenham (of all the places it had to be Cheltenham). 'I want you to know you are going to win tomorrow. I have followed your wonderful club all along, and you have nothing to worry about as the cup is yours. To be honest I think I have fallen in love with your club, and I have written a little song for you all. Would you like me to sing it?' She was absolutely enchanting, and who could refuse such an offer? It has been so many years that although I can recall the conversation the song itself now eludes me. But sing it she did, and it was a pleasant little ditty obviously thought out with care and consideration. Before going, she thanked me for listening and then reminded me not to worry as the cup was coming to Plough Lane tomorrow evening.

The Squad and Statistics

Dave Beasant

Position: Goalkeeper

Date of birth: 20 March 1959

Birthplace: Willesden

Height: 6ft 4in

Signed from: Edgware, £1,000

Dons debut: 12 January 1980 v Blackpool

Clive Goodyear

Position: Defender

Date of birth: 15 January 1961

Birthplace: Lincoln

Height: 6ft

Signed from: Plymouth Argyle, £45,000

Dons debut: 29 August 1987 v Derby County

John Scales

Position: Defender

Date of birth: 4 July 1966

Birthplace: Harrogate

Height: 6ft

Signed from: Bristol Rovers, £70,000

Dons debut: 15 August 1987 v Watford

Andy Thorn

Position: Defender

Date of birth: 12 November 1966

Birthplace: Carshalton

Height: 6ft

Signed from: turned professional after completing apprenticeship

Dons debut: 6 April 1985 v Notts County

Brian Gayle

Position: Defender

Date of birth: 6 March 1965

Birthplace: Kingston upon Thames

Height: 6ft 1in

Signed from: turned professional after completing apprenticeship

Dons debut: 27 March 1985 v Shrewsbury Town

Eric Young

Position: Defender

Date of birth: 25 March 1960

Height: 6ft 2in

Signed from: Brighton & Hove Albion, £60,000
Dons debut: 15 August 1987 v Watford

Terry Phelan

Position: Defender
Date of birth: 15 March 1967
Birthplace: Manchester
Height: 5ft 6in
Signed from: Swansea City, £100,000
Dons debut: 15 August 1987 v Watford

Vaughan Ryan

Position: Midfielder/defender
Date of birth: 2 September 1968
Birthplace: Westminster
Height: 5ft 9in
Signed from: turned professional after completing apprenticeship
Dons debut: 22 April 1987 v Tottenham Hotspur

Lawrie Sanchez

Position: Midfielder
Date of birth: 22 October 1959
Birthplace: Clapham
Height: 6ft 1in
Signed from: Reading, £20,000
Dons debut: 22 December 1984 v Birmingham City

Vinnie Jones

Position: Midfield

Date of birth: 6 January 1965

Birthplace: Watford

Height: 5ft 11in

Signed from: Wealdstone, £15,000

Dons debut: 22 November 1986 v Nottingham Forest

Andy Clement

Position: Defender

Date of birth: 11 November 1967

Birthplace: Cardiff

Height: 5ft 8in

Signed from: turned professional after completing apprenticeship

Dons debut: 1 November 1986 v Tottenham Hotspur

Alan Cork

Position: Striker

Date of birth: 4 March 1959

Birthplace: Derby

Height: 6ft

Signed from: Derby County, free transfer

Dons debut: 11 February 1977 v Scunthorpe United

Terry Gibson

Position: Striker
Date of birth: 23 December 1962
Birthplace: Walthamstow
Height: 5ft 5in
Signed from: Manchester United, £200,000
Dons debut: 29 August 1987 v Derby County

John Fashanu

Position: Striker
Date of birth: 9 September 1962
Birthplace: Kensington
Height: 6ft 1in
Signed from: Millwall, £120,000
Dons debut: 29 March 1986 v Portsmouth

Dennis Wise

Position: Winger
Date of birth: 16 December 1966
Birthplace: Notting Hill
Height: 5ft 7in
Signed from: Southampton, free transfer
Dons debut: 11 May 1985 v Cardiff City

Carlton Fairweather

Position: Winger
Date of birth: 22 September 1961

Birthplace: Dulwich
Height: 5ft 11in
Signed from: Tooting & Mitcham United, £13,000
Dons debut: 1 January 1985 v Oldham Athletic

Laurie Cunningham

Position: Winger
Date of birth: 8 March 1956
Birthplace: Archway
Height: 5ft 10in
Signed from: Charleroi, free transfer
Dons debut: 20 February 1988 v Newcastle United

Robbie Turner

Position: Striker
Date of birth: 18 September 1966
Birthplace: Easington
Height: 6ft 3in
Signed from: Bristol Rovers, £15,000
Dons debut: 19 December 1987 v Norwich City

Andy Sayer

Position: Striker
Date of birth: 6 June 1966
Birthplace: Brent
Height: 5ft 9in
Signed from: turned professional after completing apprenticeship
Dons debut: 27 August 1983 v Bolton Wanderers

Ian Hazel

Position: Midfielder
Date of birth: 1 December 1967
Birthplace: Wimbledon
Height: 5ft 11in
Signed from: turned professional after completing apprenticeship
Dons debut: 4 November 1987 v Liverpool

Paul Fishenden

Position: Striker
Date of birth: 2 August 1963
Birthplace: Hillingdon
Height: 6ft
Signed from: turned professional after completing apprenticeship
Dons debut: 3 November 1981 v Portsmouth

Paul Miller

Position: Striker
Date of birth: 31 January 1968
Birthplace: Woking
Height: 6ft
Signed from: turned professional after completing apprenticeship
Dons debut: 15 August 1987 v Watford

Simon Tracey

Position: Goalkeeper

Date of birth: 9 December 1967

Birthplace: Woolwich

Height: 6ft

Signed from: turned professional after completing apprenticeship

Dons debut: No appearances prior to 1988 FA Cup Final

Kevin Bedford

Position: Defender

Date of birth: 26 December 1968

Birthplace: Carshalton

Height: 5ft 8in

Signed from: turned professional after completing apprenticeship

Dons debut: 31 October 1987 v Tottenham Hotspur

John Gannon

Position: Winger

Date of birth: 18 December 1966

Birthplace: Wimbledon

Height: 5ft 8in

Signed from: turned professional after completing apprenticeship

Dons debut: 8 May 1986 v Bradford City

Peter Cawley

Position: Defender

Date of birth: 15 September 1965

Birthplace: London

Height: 6ft 4in

Signed from: Chertsey, undisclosed fee

Dons debut: No appearances prior to 1988 FA Cup Final

Third round

Saturday, 9 January

Wimbledon 4 (Fashanu 44, Wise 54, Turner 71, Fairweather 90) West Bromwich Albion 1 (Thorn og 86)

HT: 1-0

Attendance: 7,252

Wimbledon: Beasant, Goodyear, Phelan, Jones, Gayle, Thorn, Fairweather, Cork, Fashanu, Sanchez, Wise (Turner).

WBA: Powell, Dickenson, Cowdrill, Palmer, North, Kelly, Hopkins, Goodman, Reilly, Burrows, Williamson.

Referee: M. Bodenham

Fourth round

Saturday, 30 January

Mansfield Town 1 (Kent 67) Wimbledon 2 (Cork 43, Phelan 60)

HT: 0-1

Attendance: 10,462

Mansfield: Hitchcock, Graham, Garner, Lowery, Foster, Coleman, McKennon (Stringfellow), Ryan, Cassells, Kent, Charles.

Wimbledon: Beasant, Goodyear, Scales, Jones, Gayle, Thorn, Wise, Cork, Fashanu, Sanchez, Phelan.

Referee: H. Taylor

Fifth round

Saturday, 20 February

Newcastle United 1 (Cork og 58) Wimbledon 3 (Gibson 6, Gayle 57, Fashanu 85)

HT: 0-1

Attendance: 28,759

Newcastle: Kelly, Anderson, Wharton, McCreedy, P. Jackson, Roeder, McDonald, Gascoigne, Goddard, Mirandinha, D. Jackson (O'Neill).

Wimbledon: Beasant, Goodyear, Phelan, Jones, Gayle, Thorn, Gibson, Cunningham (Cork), Fashanu, Sanchez, Wise.

Referee: J. Worrall

Quarter-final

Saturday, 12 March

Wimbledon 2 (Young 49, Fashanu 73) Watford 1 (Allen 19)

HT: 0-1

Attendance: 12,228

Wimbledon: Beasant, Goodyear, Phelan, Jones, Gayle, Thorn, Gibson, Cork (Young), Fashanu, Sanchez, Wise.

Watford: Coton, Gibbs, Rostron, Jackett, Morris, McClelland, Sterling (Roberts), Allen, Blissett, Porter, Hodges.

Referee: N. Midgley

Semi-final

Saturday, 9 April (White Hart Lane)

Wimbledon 2 (Fashanu 54 pen, Wise 80) Luton Town 1 (Harford 48)

HT: 0-0

Attendance: 25,963

Wimbledon: Beasant, Scales, Phelan, Jones, Young, Thorn, Gibson (Cunningham), Cork, Fashanu, Sanchez, Wise.

Luton: Dibble, Breacker, Grimes (Black), McDonough, Foster, Donaghy, Wilson, B. Stein, Harford, M. Stein, Johnson.

Referee: K. Hackett

Final

Saturday, 14 May (Wembley Stadium)

Liverpool 0 Wimbledon 1 (Sanchez 36)

HT: 0-1

Attendance: 98,203

Liverpool: Grobbelaar, Gillespie, Ablett, Nicol, Spackman (Mølby), Whelan, Beardsley, Aldridge (Johnston), Houghton, Barnes, McMahon.

Wimbledon: Beasant, Goodyear, Phelan, Jones, Young, Thorn, Gibson (Scales), Cork (Cunningham), Fashanu, Sanchez, Wise.

Referee: B. Hill

Statistics

	Liverpool	Wimbledon
Goal attempts	17	9
Shots on target	8	2
Shots off target	5	4
Headers on target	1	1
Headers off target	3	2
Corners	8	3
Offside	2	6
Free kicks	23	11
Throw-ins	29	18
Yellow cards	0	0
Red cards	0	0
Penalties	1	0
Goals	0	1

Acknowledgements

WHEN WRITING a book it comes in phases. The pitch, the acceptance, the drive, the doubt, the breakthrough, the long hours, and most of all – the support.

Just like any football team no single person can win a game, and just as in the process of writing, it is more than the person tapping away on the keys. There are many links in the chain to get things going and moving along, and the final link that brings it together. So first of all I'd like to thank the wonderful people at Pitch Publishing for believing in me and a project they had faith in. It is always a nervous moment when you put an idea forward, to wait and see if it is something worthwhile. The fact you are reading this now shows they had belief, just as the Wimbledon team did back in 1988.

From there it is gaining extra help along the way and gaining contacts that you didn't think were possible, and the fans of Wimbledon have never ceased to amaze me when I have asked for help. Some of them have contributed to a section in this book, as it is only right that they also get to remember that amazing May day. Fans of other teams also went deep into their archives to help, so from Bracknell to Bath, West Brom to Mansfield – thank you. Notable mentions to Ray Armfield, Stephen Crabtree, Gavin Blackwell, Niall Couper and John Lynch. Others have given me invaluable advice and best wishes, so I apologise if your name isn't immediately here, but please do know that you are appreciated.

Of course, when writing it means you spend a lot of time isolated and away from your normal routine. With a large family that also takes it toll, so I am fully aware that my partner and kids will be wanting me to look up from the screen a bit more, and not be as grumpy when I'm overtired from having my head down for too long. Again, their support and tolerance is appreciated.

I hope you have enjoyed the book and if you have, then please pass it on to someone else who will appreciate it, or even better, come along to Plough Lane where the next generation of stars are waiting for your support.

Thank you.

Bibliography

Dennis Wise, *The Autobiography* (Boxtree, 1999)

Bobby Gould, *24 Carat Gould* (Thomas
  Publications, 2010)

Niall Couper, *The Spirit of Wimbledon* (Cherry
  Red Books, 2003)

Wimbledon FC Centenary 1889–1989

Clive Leatherdale, *Wimbledon: From Southern League to
  Premiership* (Desert Island Books, 1995)